ANAÏS NIN

LETTERS TO LAWRENCE DURRELL

LETTERS TO LAWRENCE DURRELL
1937-1977
by
ANAÏS NIN

Edited, introduced and annotated by Paul Herron

With a foreword by Richard Pine

SKY BLUE PRESS
Germantown, Maryland

COPYRIGHT INFORMATION

ISBN: 978-0-9987246-6-9 (print)

ISBN: 978-0-9987246-9-0 (ebook)

Library of Congress Control Number: 2020935034

PERMISSIONS

ACKNOWLEDGMENTS

The Editor would like to thank the following for their help in preparing this volume for publication: Sara Herron; Richard Pine; Dr. Lee Durrell; Aaron Lisec of Southern Illinois University; Norah Perkins of Curtis Brown Group Ltd.; Benjamin Franklin V; The Anaïs Nin Trust.

This book is dedicated to the memory of Gunther Stuhlmann, whose work inspired it.

Anaïs Nin, Louveciennes, 1930s.

FOREWORD

The conflux in Paris in 1937-1938 of three "musketeers" (as they styled themselves) created a lifelong literary and emotional bond between Anaïs Nin, Lawrence Durrell and Henry Miller—a bond that, in subsequent years, would be put to the test both aesthetically and personally. An accident of what we might call geoliterature, it gives us a time capsule of literary vision, creativity and élan which was sustained throughout their writing careers.

On the face of it, it was an unlikely—but not unholy—alliance: although Nin and Miller were conducting a sexual affair, the literary styles of her *The Winter of Artifice* and his *Tropic of Cancer* were continents apart, like their own backgrounds: hers cosmopolitan, French-Caribbean and deeply cultured, his Brooklyn working-class. Into their Paris milieu, from their new home in Corfu, came Durrell, the Anglo-Indian autodidact fledgling writer, and his English artist wife Nancy. The outcome was unpredictable, even though Durrell himself, years later, saw the trio as a "confraternity."

Paris, as the letters and Paul Herron's annotations reveal, would see the publication of Durrell's *The Black Book* in 1937, Miller's *Max and the White Phagocytes* in 1938 and Nin's *The Winter of Artifice* in 1939, financed at least in part by Nancy Durrell's capital: the "Villa Seurat Series," named after the artist colony where much of their time was spent.

As Nin observes in these letters, Miller's style and approach to writing were more akin to Durrell's. They are both "violating, invading, trespassing." She calls them "virile, possessive, Barbarian". Durrell, impressed by *Tropic of Cancer*, had completed his third (and, to him, his first "real") novel, *The Black Book* and this had been greeted by both Nin and Miller, before their meeting, as cognate with their own work.

Nin acclaimed *The Black Book* as coming from "inside the mystery," as "pure poetry," applauding "the sensual, savage moments." Twenty years later, she would greet *Justine* in the same vein: "Great tactile richness [...] sudden depths of insight [...] The balance [...] between the realism and the surrealism. Surface and depth [...] an orgy of words." She wrote to Durrell: "It resuscitated the young Larry of twenty-six." This would have been a welcome recreation of the creative nexus, since she had foreseen, even at that time, that Durrell and Miller "will go one way" while she would find "another, the woman's way." She would see the two men continuing as friends, together in spirit, while she would find herself in another place.

As an avid teenage reader of Lawrence Durrell's prose, my first encounter with Nin's writing was her diary, the first (edited) volume of which appeared in 1966, when I had already consumed *The Alexandria Quartet*. It led me towards her essays such as "Eroticism in Women", "Notes on Feminism" and "In Favor of the Sensitive Man" several years before I read better-known feminist texts such as Germaine Greer's *The Female Eunuch* or Eva Figes' *Patriarchal Attitudes* (both published in 1970).

Later, discovering Nin's novels—which for me will always be, contrary to her own belief in the diaries, her supreme achievement—I realized that titles such as *A Spy in the House of Love*, *The Four-Chambered Heart*, *The Seduction of the Minotaur* and the collection *Cities of the Interior* were closely akin in their overall trajectory to Durrell's own exploration of labyrinths, inter-related narratives and, ultimately, the massive undertaking of *The Avignon Quintet* (which Nin, had she lived to see more than the first volume, *Monsieur*, would probably not have enjoyed). The themes revealed by these evocative titles indicated the "grand lines" which Durrell would later acknowledge as their common literary ground.

We can encourage ourselves to see Nin's work from that time (*The House of Incest*, *The Winter of Artifice*) as having that same energy as the more violent texts of Durrell and Miller. All of them were engaged on an assault on literary conventions and pretensions, and on the ways that the emotions could be expressed in prose. Nin recognized the virile in *The Black Book*, "the force, the vigor, the élan, the vital motion." She saw it as a "riotous joy," a "life spurt" that Durrell shared with Miller. More than that, they each saw a nexus between the emotions and the writing, between psychology and art, which had been absent from European literature since Dostoyevsky and from America since the time of Poe. When Nin wrote in her diary at that time "I am in love with a new, as yet uncreated world", it might well have been penned by any of the three, especially in Miller's *Black Spring*, the sensitive successor to *Tropic of Cancer* or Durrell's story "Asylum in the Snow."

Nin also saw that "The real healer is the artist." Even at their most destructive (she called Miller "an anarchist") each musketeer would employ the "healing quality of art."

Nin was absolutely correct when she saw in Durrell (as she told him in 1958) "a wounded man." Before that, "I see two Lawrences—one unconscious and objective, the other unconscious and internal." It was partly this duality in Durrell which caused the wound, and which he strove all his life to integrate; the other cause, as in Nin's similar case, was a lost childhood. Healing was not only the purpose of art for the reader but for the artist, too.

For all three musketeers (and not forgetting the ever-chivalric Alfred "Joey" Perlès) the central metaphor was the Womb. Miller saw *The Black Book* as "a new womb in which to continue the creative life", and when Nin read Durrell's story "Down the Styx" she told him "you have given us the WOMB once and for all." This common pursuit had its most provocative and explicit expression in the "Air-Conditioned Womb" issue of *The Booster*, the journal which the four had liberated from its owners, the American Country Club. The issue featured Nin's "The Paper Womb," later suggestively retitled "The Labyrinth."

(The fact that *The Booster* included work by William Saroyan, Hans Reichel, Brassaï, David Gascoyne, Raymond Queneau, James Laughlin, Kostes Palamas, Mulk Raj Anand, Kay Boyle and Dylan Thomas—the first five of whom were in Paris at that time—indicates the extent of the "confraternity" around the Villa Seurat.)

There is, in fact, a strong analogy between Nin's recognition of *The Black Book* and *Justine* and her own *The House of Incest* and *The Winter of Artifice*: "the dream on one side, the human reality on the other" as she recorded in her diary. In the story "Stella" in a later edition of *Winter of Artifice* we read: "This hotel room was for him the symbol of the freedom of their love, the voyage, the exploration, the unknown, the restlessness that could be shared together, the surprise, the marvelously formless and bodiless and houseless freedom created by two people in a hotel room." It predicts both the relationships of Darley and Justine, and of Darley and Melissa, in *The Alexandria Quartet* and that of Charlock and Iolanthe in *The Placebo*, the first draft of *Tunc*. And Nin's "Sabina" in *A Spy in the House of Love* forecasts Durrell's *Livia*.

Why was there such a great misunderstanding between them in the 1960s and thereafter? Why did Nin complain of Durrell's "total lack of understanding" of her work? We can overlook the spat over Durrell's unfortunate preface to the 1959 reprint of *Children of the Albatross* as a clash of artistic temperaments. More serious was her apparent belief that neither Durrell nor Miller could embrace her feminine pursuit of the world within. And why, too, was Nin so contemptuously dismissive of Durrell's later work, telling her diary that *Monsieur* featured "impossible human beings," with "words empty," lacking "the slightest insight" into neurosis, "lack of unity" and "no feeling for the metaphysical"—and yet to tell Durrell himself that it was "as magical as ever"? There was a craving for the magic of friendship: almost in the same breath that she denounced Durrell, she told him "I value the alliance of the Three *Mousquetaires* too much"—but she valued it nonetheless.

That she could be irritated by *Monsieur*, "top heavy with ideas" (which it is!), or by Durrell's "intellectual games"—the conceit on which the western narrative of the *Quintet* as a whole depends—is understandable. But Nin had also dismissed the sequels to *Justine* in the *Quartet* with equal contempt. Although she acknowledged in her diary that she was "tormented by the image of multiplicity of selves" she found it difficult to appreciate Durrell's similar anxiety in the *Quartet*.

It is possible that Nin never had the opportunity to study Durrell's idea of bisexuality as an exchange between the male side of the woman, the female side of the man, as a "four-square" relationship. If she had known this more explicitly she would have recognized it, as she had seen *Justine*, as "a male counterpart to my novels."

Writing to Wallace Fowlie in 1960 she saw the *Quartet* as "a shallow world of fraudulent relationships." The crux of their difference, as writers, was not in fact so much the way their gender dictated their writing, but in their approach to character. If the *Quintet* is replete with "intellectual games" it is because Durrell admitted "I'm rather poor on character. I don't see deeply enough into people. I tend to make them rather puppets. Ideas interest me rather more than people." For Nin, the opposite was true: insight and passion in three dimensions.

During that intense, incandescent time in Paris, it became clear that what held them together was less than what would keep them apart. In her diary Nin recorded a conversation when Durrell urged her to "rewrite *Hamlet*"—something he, Miller and Michael Fraenkel were then undertaking. To which she replied, "That is not the kind of writing I wish to do." So Durrell said "You must make the leap outside of the womb," causing Nin to realize that "We each go different ways." And in her diary, as the war precipitated her departure from Paris, she also wrote: "We all knew we were parting from a pattern of life we would never see again, from friends we might never see again. I knew it was the end of our romantic life."

There was one major reunion of the "musketeers," when Durrell spent the early part of 1974 lecturing at the California Institute of Technology (CalTech) at Pasadena and was able to visit Miller and Nin. This was an occasion when deep affection for their common interest in the role and power of literature overcame any personal difference of character or literary style. And he could invite Nin to talk with his seminar students on his last teaching day, March 16, on *Sons and Lovers*. She would have enjoyed his using the example of Lawrence (on whom she had written her own book, very early) to demonstrate that "popularization and vulgarization of psychoanalysis" had obscured the fact that mothers "knew about transference long before Freud" and that "the mothers who behave like praying mantises are themselves gravely wounded somewhere, mostly always in the failure of their marriage and often sexwise."

As Durrell said in the "eulogy" which concludes this volume, "I could not help but marvel at the frightening tenacity and singleness of purpose which drove her on, kept her on course [...] So we have lost our woman Musketeer, and the loss is psychically a heavy one for this small group of friends! She was our Aramis—the slim and delicate and aristocratic one, the born duelist."

The eulogy is suffused with the love of association, of belonging, which each of the musketeers had missed in their questing lives; it shows how much each had been in thrall to their common bonds.

When I began my study of Durrell, he wrote to me, "We are all such different writers. How to explain our sound solidarity and affection? It was not because of any identity of ideas on style, philosophy, art, etc. I was often irritated by Anaïs and she by me. YET DESPITE RESERVATIONS WE WERE QUITE UNSHAKEABLE FRIENDS AND WOULD HAVE GONE THRU FIRE FOR EACH OTHER! It is most curious. We disagreed violently on details but on the grand lines we were quite solidly linked."

So be it.

Richard Pine, Durrell Library, Corfu
Greek Independence Day, 2020

INTRODUCTION

Anaïs Nin (1903-1977) was born to parents of Cuban descent in Neuilly-sur-Seine, France. Her father, Joaquín Nin, a celebrated pianist and composer, had a European touring schedule that kept the young family on the move—besides the Paris area, they also lived in Germany and Belgium, and spent time in Cuba. In 1913, after Joaquín relocated the family to the South of France where the young Anaïs could recuperate from a near-fatal abdominal infection, Joaquín abandoned his wife Rosa for a teenaged lover, whom he would later marry. Suddenly destitute, Rosa took Anaïs and her two younger brothers (Thorvald and Joaquín Jr.) to Spain, and then New York where she eked out a living with the help of Cuban relatives. On the slow nautical journey to America, the eleven-year-old Anaïs began one of the most important diaries in literary history, more than 35,000 pages by the end of her life.

Anaïs dropped out of school at sixteen and rejected the strict Catholic upbringing Rosa foisted upon her; she married a man she called the "banker-poet," Hugh (Hugo) Guiler, in 1923 and moved with him to Paris the following year after he took a bank job there and helped support the Nin family. In Paris, Anaïs morphed from dutiful wife to erotic adventuress and avant-garde writer; this period was highlighted by her romantic and literary affair with the rogue American writer Henry Miller.

By the time she composed her first letter to Lawrence Durrell, Anaïs Nin was thirty-three years old, had been in France for more than a decade, was the author of two books, *D.H. Lawrence: An Unprofessional*

xv

Study (Titus, 1932) and *The House of Incest* (Siana Editions, 1936), and had been Miller's lover for five years. At the same time, Lawrence Durrell, a twenty-four-year-old English writer, was living in Corfu, was newly married to Nancy Myers, and was developing his literary voice partly under the mentorship of Miller.

The story behind this collection of letters begins with Miller and his revolutionary novel *Tropic of Cancer* (Obelisk Press, 1934), for which Nin had written the preface. When Durrell was given a copy in 1935 by Barclay Hudson, a mutual friend of his and Miller's, he was so impressed that he wrote Miller a fan letter; when Miller responded, the groundwork was laid for a life-long friendship that included Nin as well.

In late 1936 Miller sent Durrell a copy of Nin's "prose poem" *The House of Incest*, to which Durrell responded favorably "in spite of the technique" and the "silly title";[1] but it was Nin who initiated the correspondence by reacting enthusiastically to Durrell's prose piece "Christmas Carol," which is where this collection begins.

During the remainder of the 1930s, Miller, Nin and Durrell forged a literary alliance; they called themselves the "three musketeers," analyzing, criticizing and encouraging each other's work and eventually executing a publishing plan called the "Villa Seurat Series," named after the Montparnasse street where Miller lived and where the three often met when Durrell visited Paris in 1937-1938. With funding from Nancy Durrell, Jack Kahane of the Obelisk Press brought out Durrell's *The*

---

[1] See L.D.'s letter to H.M. (*The Durrell-Miller Letters 1935-1980*, henceforth referred to as *DML*, p. 38).

Black Book in 1937; Miller's *Max and the White Phagocytes* in 1938; and Nin's *The Winter of Artifice* in 1939, just before Kahane's death and the beginning of World War Two.

The war separated the three—Miller went to Greece for several months, staying with the Durrells for a few weeks, later touring the Peloponnese peninsula with them before he left for New York; Nin and her husband fled to New York City; and Durrell embarked on an odyssey of new locations—perhaps most notably Alexandria, Egypt—for the next several years, much of the time under the employment of the British public service. The Durrell-Miller correspondence continued during the war, but Nin's letters to Durrell ceased after she came to New York and did not resume on a regular basis until 1957. Her silence was perhaps partly due to the chaotic life she was living—feeling lost in the harshness of the New York publishing scene, and, lacking passion for her husband, she had begun a series of "minor" relationships with several men, some of whom were very young; her affair with Miller ended bitterly in 1943, and another long-term romance, with the Peruvian communist activist Gonzalo More, ended in 1946. Her silence was also, as Nin admits in her diary in 1957, a result of the guilt she felt when Durrell was in need of money during the war and she had none to give.

Nin met Rupert Pole, an out-of-work actor sixteen years her junior, in 1947. They immediately began an affair, and she accepted his invitation to drive with him to California, which initiated what she called the "trapeze life," crisscrossing the country between Guiler in New York and Pole in California. She would spend the next thirty years, with a certain degree of success, keeping each "husband" unaware of the other.

Despite her tumultuous lifestyle, Nin meticulously kept her diary and honed her fiction-writing skills. When no American publisher would take on her work, she began printing her books on an old hand-press, including a revised version of *Winter of Artifice* in 1942 and the short story collection *Under a Glass Bell* in 1944. Thanks to Gore Vidal, a friend and editor at the E.P. Dutton publishing house, Dutton brought out Nin's novels *Ladders to Fire* in 1946 and *Children of the Albatross* in 1947, among other titles. But because of poor sales she was dropped by Dutton and subsequently found it virtually impossible to get new work published by commercial firms. Nin's chaotic but dogged efforts (and Guiler's financial support) did produce sporadic results: Duell, Sloan and Pearce published *The Four-Chambered Heart* in 1950; in a convoluted process that Guiler financed, the New York branch of British Book Centre distributed *A Spy in the House of Love* in 1954; and *Solar Barque* was privately published in 1958. When Nin signed with the small press owner Alan Swallow in 1961, she finally procured a dedicated American publisher who kept her work in print and brought out new titles. Even then, however, she languished in terms of acceptance in the American literary scene, which was largely anti-thetical to her self-reflective, modernist and erotic writing style.

She had long realized that her true literary gift lay in the diary, but she struggled with presenting it in such a way that her loved ones would not be scandalized by revelations of her sexual and emotional liaisons. Finally, in 1966, Harcourt Brace Jovanovich released the first volume of *The Diary of Anaïs Nin*, which covered the Paris years between 1931 and 1934, and in which her intimate life was edited out. The timing was right: the budding youth and second-wave feminist movements responded passionately to the account of a seeming independent woman forging a deep and meaningful life at a time when few women did. Suddenly, Anaïs Nin, at sixty-three years of age, was a sensation and in demand on the college lecture circuit.

Durrell, who worked for the British Foreign Office throughout much of the war and beyond, doing his writing in his spare time, reached his own critical and commercial success in 1957 with the release of *Justine*, the first novel of what would be known as *The Alexandria Quartet. Justine* impressed Nin so much that she resumed her correspondence with Durrell.

The post-*Justine* years included not only a resuscitated correspondence, but also the first face-to-face meeting in nearly two decades at Villa Louis, Durrell's primitive first home in Sommières. (The reunion is described in Nin's letters to Guiler and Pole, which are included here.)

As the *Quartet* novels kept appearing, Nin's opinion of the writing began to wane, even to the point where she declared that Durrell was "a brilliant cheat who does not have a deep knowledge of character" after the release of *Balthazar*, the second installment. Nonetheless, desperate to publicize her novels, she asked the now-famous Durrell to write a preface to an upcoming English edition of *Children of the Albatross*; this presented Durrell with several problems: he was in the midst of working on the

Quartet and needed time, peace and quiet; *Children* was a difficult novel for him to preface; and Peter Owen, the publisher, was in a rush and expressed impatience with Durrell. Not surprisingly, the preface did not measure up to what Nin had hoped for. If there was anything she expected from her peers, it was an understanding of her work; anything short of that she considered a betrayal. As late as December 1973, nearly fifteen years after the fact, Nin wrote in her diary: "The deep disappointment at finding out Durrell does not understand me or my work."

Another sticking point between Nin and Durrell in the later years was his belief that Hugh Guiler was a rich "patron of the arts," something Nin vehemently denied, as her letters attest.

But when Nin became critically ill with cancer in the mid-1970s, her attitude towards Durrell softened and the two enjoyed a resumption of their long and complex friendship when Durrell taught at CalTech and invited Nin to participate in his final seminar. Durrell's touching letter to Rupert Pole, written just after Nin's death in 1977, is a testament to his own warm feelings.

While many of Nin's letters can be found in her archive, most of Durrell's are not. Whenever possible, brief but pertinent excerpts from the known Durrell letters are included here. Diary entries and letters from Nin to others are included for the sake of context.

Editing of the letters was done only for the sake of clarity and the avoidance of excess repetition. Footnoting is intended to inform the reader of circumstances surrounding the letters and to identify, whenever possible, persons, situations and publications mentioned.

Brackets are used to indicate editorial additions, such as translations, dates and locations, and brackets with ellipses indicate editorial omissions of text.

Several of Nin's 1930s letters to Durrell were collected by Gunther Stuhlmann and published in Volume 5 of his *ANAIS: An International Journal* (1987; henceforth referred to as *AIJ5*). Some were excerpted in Nin's unexpurgated 1937-1939 diary *Nearer the Moon* (1996; henceforth referred to as *Moon*) and Volumes 2 (1934-1939) and 6 (1955-1966) of *The Diary of Anaïs Nin* (1967 and 1976, respectively). The rest appear in print here for the first time.

Paul Herron, Germantown, Maryland
July 29, 2020

PART ONE: PARIS AND THE WAR

1937-1946

Lawrence and Nancy Durrell, 1930s.

[Paris] January 3 [1937]

To Lawrence Durrell:

Had such a strong impression reading your "Christmas Carol"[2] that I find it hard to write about it. Yet I want you to know that you have done something amazing, reached a world so subtle, almost evanescent, caught a climate so fugitive—the fairytale, the dream, the life directly through the senses, the odor of fantasy pure, the clairvoyant phrase—beyond the weight of words, music and the rhythm. Beyond the law of gravity, chaos and the sounds of invisible accidents. A language which is shadowy and full of reverberations. Magical phrases like those used in incantations. The *mystery*. You wrote from *inside* the mystery, not from outside. You wrote with closed eyes, stuffed ears, inside the very shell. Caught the essence, this thing which we pursue in the night dream, and which eludes us, the incident which evaporates as we awake, this you caught.

You will see when you get *The House of Incest* that I tried to get there. You'll see that some of the same sensations disturbed us. I am going to sit quietly sometime, after the first chaos which was produced by your rhythm, and tell you about these phrases that I consider so deep in meaning.

I have a confession to make. I have read your letter[3] to Henry [Miller] and so I know you. Reading "Christmas Carol" made me want to throw my *House of Incest* into

---

[2] A prose piece later published as "Asylum in the Snow."

[3] Most likely written in December 1936; see *DML*.

the Seine. Too heavy—too heavy. Durrell travels faster and lighter. He danced on an echo.

Admiringly,

Anaïs Nin

[Paris, January 1937]

To a Serenader [L.D.]:

I thank you for seeing Henry as a *whole*. Few people do. They nibble at him. Your letter to him and about him was the only one I ever really liked. It was strong in its vision.

All you say about *House of Incest* is true, but for the *H of I* I don't always write with that detachment. That is the black poison culled from the *greatest attachment*—to people, truth, reality as seen without vision (we have days without vision even when one lives inside the meaning) and this other face, the opposite to the *H of I*, is a diary of fifty volumes! The roots, the peaty soil, the water, the blood and flesh, the stutterings and the purely human growls, exceed the quintessence...without conquering. Thus I believe in the common reality transformed. I believe as you believe. But what you got in the *H of I* was the smoke. (Henry says: "the neurotic fulgurations.") If you wish I'll send you the fifty volumes. (This is rather meant to put you in a real panic.) Yes, I want to change the title too. Facing a title for me is facing the impossible. I feel life and creation as an orchestra, a constellation. A title is an absolute. It terrifies me, because I worship the absolute. I hold many strings, but I have a fear of signatures. It has something to do with magic. To conjure or not to conjure. I live, feel, write

2

music. A title is a word—the word. It may dispel the evil spirits and it may also make them too real. My titles will always be bad, maybe because I'm not a writer. Henry is the real writer. I am just breathing. I breathe with fins, "antennas." How I used words—so definite—when my element is fluid, I don't know. A title, the ultimate catalyzer, is an event. It reminds me that my communication with past, present and future is so vivid I can never begin or end. I can never remember dates, ages. They are the titles. As soon as I am, or write, something I see, the metamorphosis [occurs] so quickly that the title disappears. This *is* a sea. Or a dream. A title is an act of violence and positivism. Do you know [Pedro] Calderón's *Life Is a Dream*?

Perhaps someday you might take sides on a problem unsolved, the only one Henry and I differ on—continuously. I pass from the human, soft, truthful, improvised diary to the stratosphere or the asylum—from the least artificial to the artificial. I use a pair of rusty scissors. I clip the painted *mandragores* [mandrakes]. Duality. Henry says: close the diary, the transformation will happen inside—but I say my untransformed work is better. They hamper each other. The immediate destroys the other—and you get smoke.

Why I ask you this, I don't know. Maybe because I felt that the scissors had given you a fragment.

From the very first I liked [your] heraldic world. Behind it I sensed faith, symbol, the meaning. The opposite of narcissism, since each one must be himself plus the symbol, a greater himself. The opposite of neurosis, since each one must see his part in a whole, with faith. Nobility, which aureoles the word, I take as an integrated quality. A lion, all lion, as [D.H.] Lawrence would say. Not hermaphrodism. Quality. Intactness. Gift. "Heraldic" (I am only analyzing its flavor—I never read your definition) seems to have a law of spiritual gravity. Its convolutions in space are cosmic, not in the circus. Am I right? Anyway it is a word with a magic, a secret glow to it. [4]

Anaïs

[Paris, March 1937]

Notes on *The Black Book*:[5] Because you have the gift for quintessence it is unnecessary to speak of the whole, which you give. I see the book as a banquet, a Dionysian feast, so rich that one has to eat slowly. It is amazingly rich. That is the first impression. Dazzled. One feels like the Chinese scholar who takes off his glasses before a woman as a symbol of her dazzlingness. Dazzlingness first then. The poetic quality. The fever and the intensity magnificent. The simultaneous gift of vision, of analysis and the *mystery*. Passionate analysis, that is the poetry of today. We are all drunk on the book. Without hangover. Caviar all the time, and for me the feeling of great

---

[4] L.D.'s "Heraldic Universe" was conceived in Corfu and became a lifelong motif of his imaginative world, which was a place of silence where time is suspended, "the exact moment of creation...the 'mandala' of the poet or the poem."

[5] L.D. had sent H.M. the only manuscript of his novel *The Black Book* and told him to "pitch it into the Seine" if it didn't meet his approval. H.M. and A.N. subsequently went about the monumental task of typing the book up and making plans for publication in Paris. See *DML*, p. 25.

emotion imprisoned in brilliance, in scales. Light. Not in the English sense, the light of the myth. The pages on the myth I love. Touched by the theme of the spiritual climates. The honesty of the self-analysis. The sensual savage moments, the mystery. The mystery, strangely enough, is preserved in spite of the powerful awareness. The awareness, that is superhuman, the poet. Power. Power. Power. Because the material is physical and the transformation mythical. A large universe, without horizons.

You will have to let me read the book again—I was told to hurry. It has to be sent away. I need it before my eyes. Also, the fumes of the drunkenness must dissipate. You should be glad to make people read like that. That is the rarest power today. You have the temperature, the degree of fever. When you analyze your self, the part of you which will not act on an impulse, it sounds like a paradox. Do you know the Spanish dancing that is all done on a small square, maximum of intensity, of fever, on a small space? The life in the book seems to come from that, from the turmoil; and the motion, in the end, is equal to the impulse, the turmoil, the flights into myth, the englobing, encompassing fever. Individually you may not dance; collectively you do, you dance all the time. No paralytic there; no, a kind of volcano.

I wonder whether you do not mistake the lightning-like pause during which you watch the life obliquely, the reflection in the mirror, as THE pause—that moment which even in the book proves to be like a shadow, slightly longer than the real body, which terrifies you. If there were not the chapter of self-analysis in the book no one would know *that you ever stop*.

My impression was that this part of self-analysis was the Pandora box that should not have been opened. I do not mean that it is not an ideologically perfect piece, which [David] Edgar[6] and Henry have enjoyed, and which I enjoyed, but that was my feeling that it was only this pause, this watching, this suspended vision, this long glance at the mirror alone, which broke the rhythm we call salvation. The cosmic flow and rhythm of the book itself, its unity and perfectly coordinated physical gestures, *was* the impulse; all the impulse is in the book, the potential impulse, the force, the vigor, the élan, the vital motion.

Difficult to enter this citadel without flaws...difficult to describe the way it takes hold of one. But what is important is that it seems to answer your own definition of a book, the underlined one. (To be continued.)

Anaïs

[P.S.] Received "Zero"[7] and will write you about it—soon.

[Paris], March 31 [1937]

The first notes I made on *The Black Book* were too tense. Tonight, sitting under the lamplight, Henry painting water colors, the stove so red, the atmosphere is too slack, which is better perhaps. No more timidity. I feel that I know you. What really caused the slackness was the word *faith*. It's one of my favorite words. It's the

---

[6] A painter and friend of H.M.

[7] A companion piece to "Asylum in the Snow"; the two would often be published together.

only coin I recognize, deal with, beyond races...and which makes all things warm. The stove so red: faith. So we're all sitting around the table sharing faith. No more gratitude. Recognition. I suddenly saw all kinds of things. I saw life, the warm and the very near, keeping a rhythm with you, one of retreat, receding, vanishing and then to swallow you on its given voracious rush back. Near and far. Saw that was the pain, this tide, tantalizing—sometimes causing terror and the frozen pages of *House of Incest*. I'm grateful to you for seeing the flow going out to life, and for seeing the color. The answer is the diary and other unpublished novels (one about Henry).[8] And you causing this questioning of the semblance, before the mirror.

"Zero" I warmed to a little less than the "[Christmas] Carol" but it has the same white heat quality and mystery. The mystery in all you write is important...that which the power of analysis usually destroys; the poet in you creates constantly; all that bursts out is pure poetry and mystery. Intact. In both pieces there is that fine simultaneous *vision and veiling* in the same breath. That proclaims the strength of the poet. The tragic fate of those who unveil, who open the Pandora box, without the power to summon new demons, new perplexities, new emotions, will surely be spared you. To merely unveil is tragic. To create is joyous. That is the riotous joy you and Henry share, and I with you. In all you write there is that life spurt, a marvelous incandescence.

---

[8] A novella later incorporated into *The Winter of Artifice* (1939) with the title "Djuna."

I regret that Henry is such a vitiated city man, cannot live without the café, the movies, and a crowd passing by, or we might have come down [to Corfu]. I like the kind of life you lead. I like that intensity inside of one, and the outer world nourishing one with softness, light, air, water. The city gives nothing. Anemia. But Henry says the soul thrives on garbage cans...on a little dirt. Too bad. I have great desires to leave the city, after a whole year of typing, writing, copying, talking, and sensuality as the only nourishment. And what a lot we would have to say.

Thank you for "Zero," and for all you have said about my writing. My greatest weakness is this need of others' faith, the need of reassurance. I am really grateful for that.

Anaïs

[Paris, March 1937]

Henry says: leave [*The Black Book*] alone. He is against altering it. The conflict makes me uneasy. I run away. I go to the surrealist movies—a set of them. One marvelous film, like charcoal or smoke drawings, Goyaesque figures, phantasmagorical. The screen itself seemed made of a painter's "*toile*." The coarse grain, blurred quality.

This is a Club which keeps [showing] old films. A group of men in black...standing in a mystic circle. Changing places but with the motions of a scarecrow, and one of them sunk in sand up to the waist, paddling in it. All made of drawings—no reality.

Tonight—Jolas. Never saw him. I'm going to show him your Heraldic Madhouse.[9]

You're right about "cosmic" moments. Slotnikoff is merely plastic imitative, but he has sold his book and is coming to Paris. I took care of him once when I was playing at being an analyst. [10]

I wonder *where* you are now, metaphorically speaking. I'm in the night, looking for silence. The head quiet, and everything else, all the other cells and tentacles, breathing. Wonder why you called me "the submarine superwoman." That made me laugh, yet it is *accurate*. Only it took me many years to recover my fins and my swimming stride. I was trying to *walk* (like the *pingouins*?) and to think like man. I was very impressed by man's thinking (Otto Rank was my friend)...this little cancer in our heads.

Moricand[11] [was] telling us about the auction sale of all his belongings, how he suffered, how the rapacious-

---

[9] A.N. is suggesting showing *The Black Book* to Eugène Jolas (1894-1952), American writer and editor of the experimental literary journal *transition*, which was published in Paris between 1927 and 1938.

[10] Will Slotnikoff, American essayist and mutual friend of H.M. and Michael Fraenkel, was one of A.N.'s clients during her stint as amateur psychoanalyst under the tutelage of Otto Rank in New York. A Freud protégé and author of *Art and Artist*, Rank (1884-1939) was A.N.'s psychoanalyst and lover from 1934 to 1936.

[11] Conrad Moricand (1884-1954) was a Swiss-born writer and astrologer befriended by A.N. and H.M. in Paris; H.M. wrote about him in *A Devil in Paradise* (1956), and Moricand was the model for A.N.'s "Marcel" character in her erotica. At A.N.'s

ness, lust and Jewishness of people fighting over his drawings, paintings, books, intimate belongings, souvenirs, trophies, symbols, magic gifts, tokens of love and hatred, these people bartering with cupidity, calcinated him, he said, like those trees one sees in the South still standing but with their entrails burnt out, ashes. Perhaps it is true, he said, that those who unveil have tragic fates. The Husband held the tiny Siamese cat, baptized "Pépé le Moko"[12] for his apache instincts, and Bravig Imbs[13] said: "The Siamese are an exaggerated cat." The Husband answered: "I have an exaggerated wife." [Nikolai] Evreinoff, the Russian *metteur en scène* and playwright, said: "In this Petrograd school one taught to conceal the outward marks of timidity. For example, a singer, instead of twisting her hand was taught to twist her toe." And he pointed down to his own toe. I concealed the outward marks of timidity under Oriental smoothness when Jolas came in, and immediately talked to him about "Gregory."[14] He listened with great attention because he is bitterly disappointed about the poets who have turned temporal and political. He wants to start a new review with a metaphysical direction. So will Gregory please send me stuff? I may show [Jolas] *The Black Book*. But have you more short

---

suggestion, Moricand cast a horoscope for L.D. and Nancy in 1938.

[12] A name possibly inspired by the 1937 gangster film of the same name by Julien Duvivier.

[13] American novelist and poet who worked for the Paris division of *The Chicago Tribune*.

[14] Central character in L.D.'s *The Black Book*.

things to send me? Jolas says he experienced terror when reading *The House of Incest*. Evreinoff says: "It is venomous." Pray for the printing machine.[15]

Anaïs

In April 1937, Durrell wrote to Nin: "I feel a pig if I don't write and tell you what a splendid writer you are—though of course you know. It was that last thing you sent, the Dionysian little Birth scene.[16] That rang a bell *and* returned the penny: as you know, only a real heavy's strength will do that...I have always dreamed up a sort of hypothetical goal which the woman writer would reach..." (*Moon*, p. 22)

In June 1937, Durrell wrote to Nin: "I have no doubt, not a shadow of doubt about you as an artist. The sense of dislocation proves that to me more fully! Loneliness is the password..." (*Moon*, p. 35)

[Paris, June 1937]

If one told [the story of] the course of a letter: Yours came and was laid on the table by the Breton maid, between one from China and another I sent to Mallorca a

---

[15] Early in 1937, H.M. had advanced the idea of investing in a sort of mimeograph that could reproduce typed copy in different colored inks, for various self-publishing projects.

[16] A reference to the short story "Birth," based on A.N.'s late-term abortion, which was portrayed as a stillbirth in A.N.'s *Under a Glass Bell* and *The Diary of Anaïs Nin*.

year ago—returned to sender. The table has deep ridges like the sand on the beach, color of sand. I did not read the letter immediately because the Husband was there, and someone we call "Rimbaud *gai*," according to the astrologer, Moricand, who talks like Venus, Queen of the Bees, and like Maldoror[17] and the people in *House of Incest* (I collect them).

When I read [the letter], the word FAITH loomed immense and I was struck with the warmth, the summer-like softness of the letter. When I read "spiritual atrophy of Gregory" I said: no—the only trouble with Gregory is the emotional conflict, the English conflict. It's feeling— of which England is ashamed, which bothers Gregory. Difficult to say all this in English. The taboos on feeling. I don't mean that Gregory is English, god no, nor has he atrophied feelings, no, but they are curled, coiled, indirect, they move obliquely, they romp in the dark, they manifest themselves perversely, through irony, hysteria, and fully in the ecstasy. That is what is entirely lacking in [Aldous] Huxley, and why I see no affinity whatever. Huxley is no poet to begin with. *Ça ne chante pas*. And YOU DO.

Why Spandrell[18] must commit a crime is because to leap out of paralysis, created by the idea, people jump into crime—blood. Emotion is again left out. Sensation is mistaken for it. See the leap from surrealism to revolu-tion, war. Gregory, because he analyzes, is aware,

---

[17] Main character of *Les Chants de Maldoror* (1874) by Comte de Lautréamont.

[18] A character in Aldous Huxley's novel *Point Counter Point* (1928).

dedoublé [split], but he is no paralytic. His instincts, nature, are alive. His feeling flies like an explosive. It is permitted to show its face in ecstasy. At other times it is blinded, dazzled, muted by the vision. I could say to you what Henry said about me in the diary: eyes too open. And I see yours are closing a bit—the metamorphosis. You are already somewhere else. You reached life by divination first, I take it, as I reached it. How much I like Gregory and his sincerity, and his *cosmic* reachings. I tell you, few, very few, have the cosmic tentacles, the power to feel beyond and all around the reef. I object to any comparison with Huxley.

Was interrupted by the discovery of a *printing* machine for only 2,000 frs. *Printing.* What we could do with this. I have to get it somehow. I may sell my Mallorcan Arabian bedstead to a Spaniard who wants it, and get the machine. I must get it. We could do all the things nobody wants. Wait and see. I'm always dreaming of some moneyless, disinterested communication, as in the Middle Ages. No profit. Just reading and enjoying.

I'm mailing you my two unpublished novels.[19] They are old—1934-35. Please remember this. When the diary volumes return from America-England, as I am sure they will, I'll mail them to you. Don't be overimpressed by Henry's description.[20] He has magnified it. It's imperfect, tremendously so.

---

[19] A.N. is referring to the novellas "Djuna" and "Lilith," which were later incorporated into *The Winter of Artifice* (1939).

[20] H.M.'s essay on A.N.'s diaries, "Une Être Étoilique," would appear in the October 1937 issue of T.S. Eliot's journal *The Criterion.*

You can do whatever you like with the child birth [story]. It is a part of the diary. Henry made me send it to [James] Laughlin [of New Directions]. He is the only one who has it. It's part of the diary written out. That is now my problem: should I write out the diary (often like a sketch book) or forget it, create anew. I'm a prisoner of it.

[Anaïs]

[Paris, July 1937]

Dear Lawrence:

Got your postscript (was that to Henry's letter, or to a letter from you I did not receive?). Was deeply joyous at all you said about the novels. When I sent them to you I was discouraged. I had just read them with severe eyes. I thought the Father manuscript creaked with artifice and unnaturalness.[21] I was obsessed with stylization, with the Japanese painting idea. Henry and I wondered if you did not recognize "Rab," later changed to "Hans."[22] Nothing in your letter revealed whether you did or not. We were amused because we know there is a great difference between Henry the writer and the image he creates of himself, and the Henry I see. All [that] you write about the woman's crucifixion, the rift, living through man, etc., is far from rubbish. It is deeply true. It is *the* conflict. It is deeply true that woman is more hurt by the snapping of the cord. It is true that it is more difficult for her to possess her own

---

[21] A reference to the novella "Lilith," which was based on A.N.'s relationship with her father, Joaquín Nin.

[22] Hans (formerly Rab) was a thinly veiled character based on H.M. in "Djuna."

soul, as Lawrence put it, and that when she is an artist, it becomes a tragedy. If she is very feminine. And I am. You need have no fear of meeting me. I am the kind of woman no one imagines capable of writing, of doing all I have done, of handling a red hot poker, of having a soul of her own. If I get timid I vanish altogether. Nothing awesome about me, I assure you. But one thing I must tell you, the manuscripts you read are *not* the diary. That is what I think is wrong with them. I am only natural in the diary. These are the efforts to escape from the diary.

Was writing the other day about the white hysteria of the poet and the red-foamed one of women. Then heard there is a sickness called "white hysteria," up in the North of Russia. People get white hysteria from too much snow. Immediately associated this idea to your snow obsession in *The Black Book*, one which struck me very much. Snow seems to haunt you. It is one of the most seductive notes in the book, snow and loneliness. Again, man can bear the loneliness and woman cannot. She is a coward. She can't bear it.

I took *The Black Book* away from Villa Seurat, brought it home with me and am going to taste it with leisure.

About stylization: Pierre Brisson[23] says that symbolical, stylized language impedes the human participation. That is not the case with you, although you are the most transcendental writer I know. That is, with you, every word has its transcendental meaning, I feel. I can see the cuts you made were exactly right, just the excrescences. What a richness you have, and a wonderful proportion

---

[23] Editor of *Le Figaro*.

between the physical and poetic, between the Byzantine surface brilliancy and deep meaning.

What Jolas writes is not good, but he has an interesting little book on the "Language of Night" [1932]. Very Germanic, Wagnerian, full of myth and fogs, and grandeurs, and then as the catalyzer of *transition* he served the writers who were out of line.

You write a bit as if you had not received my letter about the astrologer, the cat, etc. A propos of the cat "Pépé le Moko," he can't stand being alone. We say it is neurosis, but the cat hates to be alone, and he likes to lie in boxes and he is quite healthy. He likes baskets, boxes, drawers and often gets locked up with the diaries when I work with the open velvet chest from Fez.

Henry tells me you might come in September. That will be marvelous. Marvelous. Perhaps I can hunt around and find you a free place, so you can spend what you have on other things. I will do all I can among the people who are away at that time. I like Nancy without knowing her. I sort of feel her around you, in your work, in the sky, in the sea, in the air around you.

The cable you received means your *Black Book* will be published? I rejoice over that. If it is not done we will do it with our hands, believe me. It has got to be read. It is the only vital book I have read for many years.

Now I have seen Henry and he tells me your book will not be printed, and that he wants to show it to Kahane. So I must return it quickly. I read it all through today, received the same impression as the first time, chiefly of power. Power. Deep, vital, rich soil one can dig into, find everything in it. I do not agree with the cuts you made at the end. I think there you cut some soft parts, good ones. To my mind, what needs to be cut is where the abstractions grow out of proportion to the soil, the body, the drama. Poetry, I feel, can be allowed to cast a shadow far greater than the core which set it off, but abstractions, the dancing of the skeleton, if it becomes a dance of words, is dangerous.

It's funny, I agree with all the moods; I mean they are familiar. I like the moods, the earth in it, the philosophy. There is a MAN. And very few, very few, are MAN in their books. It is a man sacking, violating, invading, trespassing and possessing all he touches. That you have in common with Henry, and it is a quality I have a great admiration for. I say it is virile, it is possessive, it is Barbarian; it is not only the vision, the seeing, the sensitive senses, but the appetite, the lust and the devouring I like. It is *active*. The whole book gives me that feeling, of electricity, warmth, currents, possession and satisfaction. You pursue the ghostly, and that you grasp too; it is satisfying that way. That's why it is fecundating. The cycle is complete, the activity has a fulfillment; it is not masturbating, it is whole. Yes, it is the book of a Man. It is mature, and as delicate as it is savage.

Anaïs

P.S. If Kahane doesn't do it, don't worry. Henry and I will do it on our own Press. I'm writing letters. Stuart Gilbert[24] gave me a 200 frs. subscription toward production of you, Miller and self.

---

[24] An English literary scholar who published significantly about James Joyce and wrote a never-used foreword to *The House of Incest*. See *A Casebook on Anaïs Nin* (Meridian, 1974), p. 1.

In July 1937, Durrell wrote to Nin: "I wept a bit, because this is the first book [*The Winter of Artifice*] in Europe which belongs to a female artist: and it is bitter. I was not concerned so much with interplay of characters but thought all the time how female it was, how the gift was total, always, unreserved, not withheld..." (*Moon*, p. 48)

[Paris, August 1937]

Dear Larry:

Rebecca [West] will be back in her London home September 1st. 15 Orchard Court, Portman Square, W 1, London. Walbeck 3606. You can see her then. I am writing to her today.

Would you do me a favor? Try and buy me a copy of my book on Lawrence, even two copies if you find them. I want to give you one. Mr. [James] Cooney wants to see it.[25]

I've written to Djuna Barnes[26]—have you? My affection to you both.

Anaïs

Diary excerpt, August 3, 1937: I walked to Henry's studio to meet Nancy and Lawrence Durrell.[27] I saw Durrell's eyes, eyes that know everything, eyes like those of a sea

---

[25] The Woodstock, N.Y. editor of the quarterly *Phoenix*, which reprinted H.M.'s essay "*Une Être Étoilique*" (Summer 1938, Vol. 1, No. 2) and some of A.N.'s work.

[26] English author of *Nightwood*, which A.N. admired.

[27] A.N.'s date of L.D.'s arrival, August 3, conflicts with *The Durrell Log*'s note that he and Nancy arrived on August 12.

animal, both of earth, sky and water, of seer and prophet, of child and old man. What keenness in them. He sees everything. His soul sees, his body, his creative self, through those clear, clairvoyant eyes. He was as I expected him to be, soft and feminine, healthy and humorous, faun and swimmer. Immediate vision. Then I saw Nancy, a long-waisted boy with beautiful, long leopard eyes, a Greek boy. And then we talked, but it was not very necessary. (*Moon*, p. 73)

Diary excerpt, August 5, 1937: I have known Lawrence Durrell for a thousand years. He is irremediably, familiarly, immediately a friend. One can talk about everything, and at the same time there is no need of it. (*Moon, p. 78*)

Diary excerpt, August 11, 1937: I was watching Durrell. He is a little amazed at himself, as someone who discovered a disease in himself. Under the golden-tanned skin, the blond hair, the sea-bottom eyes, behind the poetic gestures, mellow and human, he has found a cataract of words, a universe of nuances, shadows, quarter tones. Not by way of neurosis did he uncover the imagination he has. He is like a sailor, a mountaineer who has been visited by revelations. There is a miracle about his creation. He is a bit amazed. He walks the familiar streets with a vague uneasiness. The wine bottle has become symbolical. This expresses all he is fighting against. He does not want to lose the warmth, the flesh, the odor, the reality. (*Moon*, p. 88)

Diary excerpt, August 14, 1937: I felt that Nancy and Larry were a little uneasy, a little lost, a little ready for flight, after ten days of the Villa Seurat and the [Café le] Dôme circus. I felt their loneliness. I asked them to come and see me last night. [...] They recoil from what I recoil from. They wanted Greece again, after walking through the slippery, greasy, putrid world of Fred [Perlès], [...] Brassaï, et al.[28] It is not moral repulsion, we said, it is heraldic.

I enjoyed hearing Larry and Nancy's contempt, sadness. Larry saying: "I can't stand idiots very long [...]." I felt less alone. I was happy. In the dark we seemed to be able to say everything. Larry was exposing his fear of "going mad" if he continued writing. (Unpublished diary)

Diary excerpt, August 1937: When they [Durrell and Miller] discussed the problem of my diary, all the art theories were involved. They talked about the geographical changes undergone with time, and that it was the product of change we called art. I asserted that such a process could take place instantaneously.

Henry said: "But that would upset all the art theories." [...]

Larry, who before had praised me for writing as a woman, for not breaking the umbilical connection, said: "You must rewrite *Hamlet*."

---

[28] Alfred Perlès (1897-1990), a writer born in Austria, was a friend and supporter of H.M.; Brassaï (1899-1984) was a Hungarian-French photographer famous for his photos of Paris at night.

"Why should I, if that is not the kind of writing I wish to do?"

Larry said: "You must make the leap outside of the womb, destroy your connections."

"I know," I said, "that this is an important talk, and that it will be at this moment that we each go different ways. Perhaps Henry and Larry will go the same way, but I will have to go another, the woman's way."

At the end of the conversation they both said: "We have a real woman artist before us, the first one, and we ought not to put her down." [...]

I am not interested in fiction. I want faithfulness. (*D2*, pp. 232-233)

In August 1937, Durrell wrote to Miller: "I fold up and give in. What she says is biologically true from the very navel strings." (*Moon*, p. 85)

[Paris, September, 1937]

Larry:

I was thinking of all you had said the other day and I wrote: "*Pages d'un journal désincarné.*" Meaning disincarnated, you see. I thought I could disembody the journal, draw mysterious aphorisms, maxims, morals out of it, I mean, for [T.S.] Eliot. Impossible. I have two more numbers [of *The Criterion*] for you to read. I hope you will call soon. You were so accurate the other day, so exactly as I had imagined you would be, and really it is humorous and lovely, this golden young Jupiter, descending abruptly into the Inferno, the inferno of his own *Black Book* and *Tropic of Cancer* and of Henry and me conjugated. Unfortunately, there is no going back, and, anyway, you could not deceive me about having been there and seen it all; it shows in your eyes. And I have a sort of prophetic hunch that, without any heavy sense of responsibility, you might pull me out of my too-dark worlds (do not fear this role; one's effect on others is beyond one's self or power to alter), and perhaps I will be the one to give you the courage of your strength, of exploding. You can talk all you want about the version of *Hamlet* I will write (and now I understand better, it was a prescription for sanity and painlessness you gave me, really, for the great classical relief from terror and pain), but what I really understood is what you give me— whatever that is I don't want to dissect, but I am grateful for it. There are no solutions; there are displacements. Something in you helped me to displace myself and I breathe better. Thank you. Maybe the old FAITH idea. What can I do for you, outside of refusing to throw the ball back? I decided long ago you were a MAN. Inside of the man there can be Peter Pan. But that is for our game, another game, which we can always go on playing.

Anaïs

P.S. Had a fine laugh over the x-ray exposé—I will show it to H.

Written before Monday's talk.

[Paris, October 1937]

Larry:

Was in bed all day, so I can't go to the Villa Seurat and will have to go tomorrow, Tuesday. Will try [to] pass by your place for tea instead of dinner. Hugh is arriving tonight. Will bring back the [book by Theodor] Fontane.[29] Just another pattern, and for the moment I find these not fecund. I think patterns and arrangements are only fecund when we get lost, when we vitally need them, when we're sinking, but otherwise they are like chess games and not vital, and they kill the experience. I feel we should pounce and devour these books only when we are really sunk in the deep sea of instincts or emotions, or choking in a drama, or suffocating in subjectivity, or in some other acute crisis, when the temperature is too high. Don't you think?

Wonder what you will think of the essay on Rank for Eliot.

I think I have made out Marika.[30] She is a NATURE woman, all right, but poisoned, deluded, and pluming herself in her ideology. She uses words that stick in her throat. Cheaply. That is why she is at once ridiculous, like a parrot, and at the same time her vigor, like Dodge's,[31] cannot be overlooked.

Worked all day. Wish I had not been so groggy last night. I had things to tell you. Maybe it was not so accidental, my kidnapping you. When I saw you with Fred [Perlès] there, I suddenly remembered all we said once about living horizontally or vertically. Maybe I was afraid, and I thought they too will live horizontally, and

---

[29] German writer most known for his novel *Vor dem Sturm* (1878).

[30] Marika Norden was the pseudonym of the Scandinavian writer Megan Vogt.

[31] Mabel Dodge Luhan, a wealthy American patron of the arts.

then, not to be left alone in my vertical world, I will throw all values to the devil and no longer stand up but start to dribble at the mouth, like Fred, and so I took you both away.

With a most vertical devotion,

Anaïs

[Paris, November 1937]

Larry:

You say your letters get no reply:

It takes always a long time for bubbles and deep sea messages to travel. The whale moves slowly, especially after a meal.

I liked [David] Gascoyne;[32] I think he is a deep sea specimen. He is full of antennas. He lives in a rarefied atmosphere. I like that. I liked your answer to my "You are impersonal." You say: "It is modesty." Your eyes sometimes do stare from a snail shell, deep-set in a maze of delicacies. I will never again say: "You are impersonal."

Here are the two first pages on Fez. Fez was the place where I went to sleep, as you rightly said I needed to. I ceased questing, lamenting, leaping, etc. I [have] tried to write about it ever since. This is the beginning.[33]

Astrologically speaking, there are many reasons for your letters, per [your] request. I enjoy them. I enjoy them. I enjoy them. I enjoy them.

---

[32] An English poet associated with the surrealists.

[33] A.N. and her husband traveled to Fez, Morocco, in 1936, about which she wrote extensively in her diary.

But I know you must work, and the *pneuma* [spirit] idea is interesting. Let me see it all when it is done.

If you see Henry, get from him the part beginning [with]: "I am afraid of becoming a saint." I had meant to send it to you with the note I am enclosing, because you know the volume [of the childhood diary] it was quintessed from. Tell me what you think when you see me.

I wish I could type faster. I would offer a cut from "Zero" for *The Booster*,[34] copy it for you. I may do it this Sunday. What struck me this time rereading *The Black Book* is the depths. This compression in you which I like immensely works very much like a poisoned arrow; one is swiftly hit and then more slowly the poison spreads in one. Arrows, arrows. Don't let anyone get you too slack or too loose. *The Black Book* is full of diamonds. No book today can bear rereading. I can never reread anyone, but this I can.

Salut,
Anaïs

---

[34] In July 1937, the President of the American Country Club in Paris had asked Alfred Perlès to take over as editor of the Club's periodical, *The Booster*, giving him free rein provided he continued to carry some of the social notes and the golf scores of the Club members. Perlès, goaded by H.M., quickly developed it into the "house organ" of the Villa Seurat circle and their friends. After four issues (September, October, November 1937, and a double issue December 1937-January 1938) the magazine was renamed *Delta* and three more issues appeared (April 1938, Xmas 1938, and Easter 1939), including an all-poetry issue under L.D.'s editorship. Somewhat scandalized by the initial content, the Club had withdrawn from the project at an early stage. (*AIJ5*, p. 84)

[Paris, November 1937]

Dear Larry:

I read "Down the Styx"[35] with amazement and wonder. You have done there an extraordinary thing, a unique thing. It arouses the strangest sensations, like those of a dream, of an obscure memory. It is concrete, fleshly and fantastic; it is monstrous and possible. The humor of the juxtaposition of "Aunt Prudence" in this world is tremendous. Humor is marvelous, and at the same time the sensual experience. You have given us the WOMB once and for all. It is really superb, because it is so vivid, so real, so clear, and at the same time instinctual; what roots you reach down into. My deepest respect and admiration. The language is beautiful, the language for the thing itself, a language of atmosphere, and tissues. I tell you, Larry, this is a piece of genius. I was thunderstruck. You have done it. You have surpassed man, woman and child itself in the completeness of the voyage, its thoroughness, its abysmal reproduction. There is something uncanny in it all; you go through sex, birth and death with eyes open. Your eyes were never closed, even in the womb; that is why the look in them always strikes me so much. I am very proud of you, very moved and admiring.

Anaïs

---

[35] "Down the Styx in an air-conditioned canoe," L.D.'s satirical-lyrical letter to his departed "Auntie Prudence," appeared in the December 1937-January 1938 "air-conditioned womb" number of *The Booster*, which also contained A.N.'s "The Paper Womb" (later titled "The Labyrinth" in *Under a Glass Bell*) and H.M.'s "The Enormous Womb." (*AIJ5*, p. 85)

P.S. I talked last night to Henry, very quietly, very gently (in my most seductive and subtle manner), about the small things, about printing short things, etc., as I promised you I would. I would have persuaded God himself, I was so tactful and delicate and really right. Henry's feathers were not ruffled. But deep down I tell you this: This constant peripheral activity is as much part of Henry's character as breathing. It is like asking him to breathe once instead of twice in one minute. I feel we can do nothing about it; at the most when an actual piece is put before us (like the "Alf" letter)[36] we may win out individually, but we will never win out on the principle. He wants his books morcelled; he feels he is active only when there is a rain of things; his whole life is the opposite of channelization, aiming at a center, shooting guns instead of hunting guns, which, you know, go off in clouds of dust bullets. I will give you all my voting power, but even last night Henry was saying: "If I had the six hundred francs in my pocket I would still do the 'Alf' letter."

Frankly, Larry, it will remain a problem. I think you should make that a clear condition of the Durrell-Miller Press proposition. Let Henry do his fragments outside the Kahane enterprise, when he gets hold of the rent

---

[36] "What Are You Going to Do About Alf?", an "open letter" composed by H.M. in September 1935, suggested somewhat facetiously that since Alfred Perlès was "always looking for a comfortable room in which to write," his friends should raise some money by subscription to send him to Ibiza so he could finish his novel *Le quatuor en ré majeur* (1938). Nothing much came of the scheme. (*AIJ5*, p. 85)

money. But do make it a condition, otherwise you will not be able to stem the tide of Henry's love of fragments.

A.

Diary excerpt, November 1937:[37] Durrell calls my copies of the diary my black children—they are bound in black—I keep them in the Arabian wedding chest; violet velvet with gold nails. Lovely to see the *coffer* open, brimming full. And now this one will go into the vault—to be locked among other people's jewels and testaments. (*Moon*, p. 168)

[Paris, November 1937]

Larry:

You read the end of the last volume of the diary, and perhaps you can better tell me if this extract from it is good or bad. Dorothy Norman[38] asked me for extracts. Do you think they can be made by this sort of disembodiment? What is your honest feeling? You know the complete pages. This quintessing may be very bad. Tell me.

Do you want me to find the parts of *The Black Book* I think you could send here?

Anaïs

---

[37] L.D. and Nancy returned to Paris from London, where they had spent three weeks, and stayed with Perlès at 7 Villa Seurat before renting an apartment at 21 rue Gazan, where they would live until mid-December.

[38] The New York editor of the avant-garde literary journal *Twice a Year*.

ACROPOLIS HOTEL [March 1938]
180, Boulevard Saint-Germain Paris VIe

My very dear generous Limpet:

I got the houseboat![39] For 500 frs.! Steam heat and bathroom and windows and everything I wanted—and it floats—and it's marvelous. I'm so happy I can't write.

However, I won't rest until I get someone to take your [apartment]. Faustino[40] wants to see it anyway and asked for a rendezvous. Would you be home Friday at tea time? I may bring an American girl—a freak, half child, half old woman with a young Negress voice.[41]

You would love the houseboat. Down the Styx feeling.

Love,

Anaïs

P.S. I keep my promise about [Hans] Reichel.[42]

---

[39] From September 1936 to July 1937, A.N. had rented a houseboat, to which Gonzalo More had given the name *Nanankepichu*, meaning in the old Inca language Quechua "not at home." When the owner sold the boat, A.N. eventually found *La Belle Aurore*, which is the subject of this letter, owned by the French actor, Michel Simon. In *The Diary of Anaïs Nin*, A.N. used the latter name for both boats. (*AIJ5*, p. 87)

[40] Princess di San Faustino was Jane Campbell (1865-1938), an American who had married into Italian nobility.

[41] The woman is most likely Thurema Sokol, whom A.N. befriended in New York.

[42] German expatriot painter (1892-1958) who befriended H.M. and A.N., about whom both wrote (H.M.'s "The Cosmological Eye" and *Order and Chaos chez Hans Reichel*; A.N.'s "The Eye's Journey").

[Paris, March 1938]

Dear Nancy and Larry:

Thinking over what Nancy told me today. I don't want you to walk out of your apt. and lose what you got, and perhaps your right to re-enter France. You leave it to me to rent for you. I am sure I can do it. Just tell me when you want and need to leave for London and leave me the key, a word to the concierge and I'll take care of it.[43] Until April 15, as I understand, there is nothing to pay. I'll try to get 3 months in advance so as to meet the April 15 payment. Will talk it over, and that will save your furniture.

Anyhow, I want you to have dinner on the boat as soon as I am settled. Hugh's plans are indefinite.[44] I will know by the middle of the week whether he's coming or whether I am to go over. If he comes you are still welcome to stay in his place with his English cousin [also visiting]—or if I go over then you might have to wait, say, until the weekend, about March 15th. Does that suit your plans? If not you can be there while I'm there. We can rent a bed if necessary. Tell me frankly what would suit you. The whale is at your service and will try to be graceful.

Love,
Anaïs

---

[43] L.D. went from Paris to London at the end of March and returned to Paris on April 8.

[44] H.G. was working in London, coming to Paris only inter-mittently.

[Paris, April 1938]

Dear Limpet:

The whale wants you to know you have the largest, most luxuriously furnished, the most palatial pearl-covered cabin on the highest deck (outside cabin), with a view of the entire ocean, on the said whale's back. In fact, this whale who seems most independent, who to all mariners' eyes seems willing enough to travel alone, would not travel anywhere without the limpet; her gay tail would limp...immediately.

The whale has put forth a new wisdom tooth (the objective attitude) and has much to report which may be turned into lamp oil, olive oil, and hair tonic.

Delighted that you sent Captain Norman[45] a few of your marine samples. The "Down the Styx" haunts me. It reminds me of a strong childhood impression of an author you perhaps never read, or perhaps did, Jules Verne. Jules Verne is not very highly regarded but I think his imagination was the best that was ever given to children to read. And one of his books was all about what happened to a party of people who went inside the earth through volcanic caverns hoping to reach the other side.[46] This story, which was a marvel to me, mysterious, bowels, entrails and all, had a potent effect on me, and one which I suppose could be explained away as the Womb, nostalgia. When I read "Down the Styx" I experienced the same magical, mysterious effect, so

---

[45] A reference to Dorothy Norman.

[46] *Journey to the Center of the Earth* (1864).

vividly. It's the reality of the fantasy, the smell and the color and the sound of it that is astonishing, the fleshiness of it, the rocks and earth of it. Everyone's womb must be different. Yours is certainly concrete, palpable, vivid. One is drugged at the same time as violently awakened. A very strange effect. Strong.

Love to you both,

Anaïs

[P.S.] I will come soon. Very soon. Have been loaded with all kinds of jobs. Wish you'd call up like Gascoyne and come. Otherwise I get pulled here and there, with Joaquín[47] sailing soon, Hugh leaving for Egypt, moving preparations and order for an abridged version of Diary from Scribner's.

Irony: just when I wanted to transform—I've been transforming.

[Paris, April 1938]

Larry:

You read the end of the last volume of the diary, and perhaps you can better tell me if this extract [from the story "Birth"] is good or bad. Dorothy Norman asked me for extracts. Do you think they can be made by this sort of disembodiment? What is your honest feeling? You know the complete pages. This quintessencing may be very bad. Tell me. Do you want me to find the parts of *The Black Book* I think you could send her?

---

[47] Joaquín Nin-Culmell, A.N.'s younger brother, was planning a move to America to take a teaching job to supplement his budding career as a composer and pianist.

Anaïs

[Paris, April 1938]

Not being used to weeping in public, we went home and dwelt on all we would miss in you and Nancy.[48] List so long as to be impossible to remember. Then the next day we went for the books. The concierge said she had heard rumors you were not coming back. I said you were. Then Henry and I picked up as many books as we could and left, and have not returned since—we rescued the Cezanne, which I am keeping for you, and *Nightwood*. The rest were mine. Too bad we could not swallow the skies, nor become globe trotters of the lamp. Perhaps tonight we have another fit of audacity. Henry suffers too much from tremens when we do these things.

Here is a letter. We sent a telegram for the typewriter. And I am mailing you the book you left.

I have not many news. The sea has been rough, due to the regular service of river boats. Symons[49] called on Henry. I have not seen him. I am working on "Chaotica."[50] I wish you would write the article about the boat. I'll send you photo of me in the boat. Marika Norden says we women are all Princesses in a Princeless world! She has megalomania. Asks me what I am doing about it. Takes it

---

[48] The Durrells abruptly left Paris April 10, 1938, leaving many of their possessions behind, possibly as a result of the deteriorating European political climate.

[49] W.T. Symons was a co-editor of the British literary magazine *Purpose.*

[50] Working title for *The Winter of Artifice.*

for granted I am in the same boat, and I have to explain, without making her too envious, that I am a satisfied female; in fact, the world is crowded with edible men. What do you think? Nancy and I have nothing to complain about.

Love to you both,

Anaïs

[Paris, April-May 1938]

Writing in a café. I asked *de quoi écrire* and they gave me one page. *Pas de quoi écrire* about *The Black Book* which is still so alive in my head. I helped Henry with some of the proof-reading—so I was able to taste certain parts more deeply. I am waiting to have a copy loaned to me. I want to write you while looking at it. Some of the phrases strike a tremendous resonance in me. They are usually the visionary phrases, charged with meaning. Yet I'm not blind to the physical beauty of the book, the sensual warmth of it—all that makes such a powerful whole out of it. That is what holds me. It's a whole, a total, an absolute. That is what you wanted, I know. That is what you got, with power. I see only one defect, and that is only due to your great riches—there is a rupture of words at times—an orgy—run amuck, they drown the experience. But what a small defect. No *organic* weakness. No germ of death in the book. No infection from the brain. All that you describe—the death—is contradicted by the tremendous birth—beauty. Problem only of proportion—due most probably to your conscious selection of what you think good—the *gem*. Sometimes the art gem is not the flame.[51] I'm sure you discarded much that was good, perhaps the wet, the soft, the lax, the fluid, the apparently not born which is sometimes *the* birth—the living page. I know. I used to be so afraid of the world, so much on the defense, I wanted to give only what they could slip and fall on, nothing they could dig their nails into.

So with writing you at first, because I was so impressed—but that's over. Strangely, it vanished while I was reading the end of *The Black Book*. In the end, which I read to be Nancy, the YOU—there is something so delicate, so profound and subtle, tender, and mystical— human, too—I can't define it. It's when writing gets more like the *touch*, like closed eyes, palate, breath... Beyond writing, you were breathing. The words were breathing. The miracle was really accomplished; words became breathing, with a strange silence, stillness, a sort of infinite suspense. To possess everything, to enclose everything, you arrived at a kind of gentle suspense, sacred like the breath...

I'm deeply grateful for what you write me about the "Birth" story, what you, Nancy, and the others feel.[52] I need that. Outside of Henry nobody else notices what I do, or cares very much. The diary is liked but feared. *The House of Incest* was sunk by the title, which was misleading. I want to write about Henry because few

---

[51] Possibly a reference to English essayist Walter Pater's quotation "To burn always with this hard gemlike flame, to maintain this ecstasy, is success in life."

[52] A.N.'s story, "Birth," appeared for the first time in the Fall 1938 issue of *Twice a Year*. (*AIJ5*, p. 89)

outside of you see him as a whole. *I know his work to come.* I have no time, no solitude, no retreat. I'm too much in the current—flowing. You can't both flow and construct. Only wrote the child thing ["Birth"], in one year. Maybe I've done enough. I will not be able to get to Corfu. Too many ties—impediments. *De quoi écrire.* Maybe it can all be put on one page. Written while waiting for life...

Thank you for your faith.

Anaïs

[Paris, May 1938]

Dear Nancy and Larry:

Henry is typing and throwing messages to you over his left shoulder: tell them...tell him...and tell him...tell him... Anyway, I gather this: the letter you wrote on the "Hamlet" book, Larry, which I was crazy about—Henry reread it and got drunk on it again and he says he's sending it to Symons of *Purpose*—will get it printed for you somehow, somewhere.[53] That he'll include it in the Brochure—that he cut out all references to Fraenkel so you need not fear he'll be hurt.

Henry ran across Gascoyne the other day. He says he will do the next proof-reading as he has the rest of the M.S. When I did half of the proof-reading with Henry I

---

[53] In January 1937, L.D. had written to H.M. about the "Hamlet" correspondence between H.M. and Michael Fraenkel, which was growing into a massive book and was published, eventually, in two volumes in June 1939 and June 1941, respectively, by Carrefour. L.D.'s letter, titled "Hamlet, Prince of China," appeared in the Xmas 1938 issue of *Delta*. (*AIJ5*, p. 90)

enjoyed it all over again—a feast. I don't understand all this you write about doing a work and postponing the writing.[54] It seems to me you should push it, on the contrary; that *this* is the moment. You've just got hold of yourself. And you can't get panicky *now*. The self, the voice that came out of you, the cosmic, the *larger* Larry, out of the depths, intimidates the young, the *lutin*, the child in you—playing with a boat. It's a conflict between the aged Tibetan speaking in his trances, and Peter Pan. You can't run away now. Nancy is certainly not the one to cause this. I know her allegiance, her all-absolving attitude. She would never want you to work at anything but this fusion of your own duality. Nancy, I know her, desires nothing for herself but that you should become *more* YOU. Your big job now is welding, alchemy—to eat the heart and liver and sex of this cosmic mythical being speaking out of you and become IT. That's what I feel.

Henry sent "Asylum in the Snow" to Cooney. I sent "Zero"—*recommandé*!

About your essay on Rank.[55] Please write to Symons about it first. You may not know he accepted my essay on "Creative Principle in Analysis" to appear in the next issue [of *Purpose*] and we had a slight controversy in which he revealed his ignorance of Rank and allegiance to [Alfred] Adler, and I'm afraid he still does not relish him. He only agreed to do mine when I said he could

---

[54] L.D. was conflicted between the "work" he did under the pseudonym "Charles Norden" (a novel, *Panic Spring*, published early in 1937) and his "writing," i.e. *The Black Book* et al. (*AIJ5*, p. 90)

[55] The essay was apparently never published.

write a *Note* saying what I attributed to Rank was originally discovered by Adler—which is utterly false, even if I never read Adler! So write him first. You ought to write the essay anyway as it could be published somewhere else.

Interruption: Henry says healing is the *easiest*, greatest delusion of man. The real healer is the artist. This healing *doctor* business is an evasion of the healing by the magic—believe me—I tried the direct healing, with the hand, the sympathy, etc. It doesn't ever work as profoundly as the "healing quality of art." Nietzsche. Read *Birth of Tragedy*. Do you know it?

The fragment [of *The Black Book*] in *Seven*[56] didn't read like a fragment but a "*bolide*" [rocket]—the hard and fast *bolide* for the trip to the Moon.

Barker's[57] book *Janus* is adolescent, romantic. I can understand him making the inadequate remark that you're "engaging."

Henry is writing—well—*Silence*. Yes, we said, music takes account of silence. Henry, when he writes as he is writing now, achieves *silence*. It is finite. Pure myth.

"Something more active in the world of people," you say, referring to Herr Doktor. But my god, it won't be people, it will be cripples. And it does not make for

---

[56] A magazine edited by John Goodland and Nicholas Moore from Taunton, England, published a number of contributions by L.D. including "Asylum in the Snow" (Volume 3, November 1938) and "Zero" (Volume 4, February 1939). It also published several contributions by A.N. (*AIJ5*, p. 91)

[57] George Barker was an award-winning English poet who contributed to A.N.'s erotica-writing scheme for a private "collector" in New York during the early 1940s.

connection. It is impersonal. A role. *No more roles for you, Sir.*

London—an eclipse. I was not in the mood. Place grated on me. I saw nobody. Got back to my boat as if I had been cut off from the very sources of life—flow. Happy again. Writing the book for you and Nancy—for the Villa Seurat series—dedicated to you.[58]

Sending back the photos. Strange to see the family. I always feel: they are not the family. Substitutes. Same old story as the Bible parents. Whoever *really* gave birth to you, one of the Atlantis personages, *hors séries*, would not acknowledge paternity. Left you in care of this family seated around you—the nurse—and left you to seek your own true origin in the myth. Poor parents chosen, betrayed in this fecundation by the divine seed, inter-cepted too late by man, who believed *his* seed made you. Where everything looks right and normal is where you laugh between the two night-black people.

Love to both of you,
Anaïs

Anaïs Nin
Péniche la Belle Aurore
Quai des Tuileries Paris 1er
[September 1938] [fragment]

[...] catching at my throat like a drowning man. It was like handling an octopus. When she left I got sick—after a month of wrestling. Then the boat was exiled from

---

[58] The Obelisk edition of *The Winter of Artifice* was dedicated to "Nancy and Larry."

Paris—to the spot where I was born [Neuilly]. That return to birth spot depressed me—like a vicious circle. My Father living a few blocks away. And now—no permission to return to Paris. I have to give it up. It rains all over my books and papers. Too far. Lonely. I didn't mean to write a sad letter. Henry is writing magnificently—you'll be proud. Marvelous. Very quiet and retired. Just writing.

I'm trying to finish "Chaotica" for Kahane. Will send you carbon. It's your book, you know.

Write me "Poste Restante—Gare d'Orsay."

I've been a little to the beach—with Hugo—and once with the "monster" [probably Thurema Sokol].

Cooney, did you know, has a violent and mysterious horoscope. I'll have yours and Nancy's done for Xmas by Moricand, if I'm in funds. He really makes a portrait.

Where are you now? I hear you have a colony there [in Corfu] just as in Paris. Jupiter. Jupiter. When is Nancy coming to give an exhibition...[59]

Love to you both,
Anaïs

[Paris, September 1938]

This is to inform Cervantes Pequeño and his Dulcinea that henceforth He Hath a Home and Hearth in London. Welcome from now on in Hugh's home, any time, there is a room for you. No extras, no luxury tax, all modern comforts, sun terrasse, etc. etc.

---

[59] Nancy was an accomplished artist; most of her work was lost during the Durrells' move from Corfu to Athens and Alexandria.

Love, Anaïs

[P.S.] Just let me know whenever you wish to stay there, when you have to pay London a visit.[60]

[Paris, November 1938]

Dear Nancy and Larry:

I swore I wouldn't write until I was out of the tunnel, not the womb this time, mind you, but the death of Europe, Paris, security, ivory towers, boats, escapes, illusions. As you said in your letter: "Anaïs can't be depressed." No, l wouldn't be living up to myself, but l was, nevertheless, and just coming out to hand you "Chaotica." Hoping, hoping you will like the new arrangement: as the last book I turned out, like all my books, was too short, I took three of them and boiled them all together, and hoping you will like it.

I am rejoicing over the review of *The Black Book*.[61] For once, they are giving you what you deserve. Very thrilled with the emphasis on the "music" which I often thought of in relation to you. You are really being re-sponded to, even if at times what they say is not exactly what you want to hear—it never is—it is meant as praise and recognition. Marvelous. Marvelous too your letter on not writing, a little gem, all you wrote about yourself

---

[60] L.D. and Nancy passed through Paris on November 19 on their way to London, where they stayed at H.G.'s apartment with A.N.; on November 29 the Durrells returned to Paris, where they were until mid-December.

[61] While which review A.N. refers to is unknown, it could very well be the favorable one that appeared in *New English Weekly*.

when you don't and can't write, you say. When are you coming to London? I am going there next weekend.

I am living now in a miniature hotel room. Reading [Emanuel] Swedenborg and [Jean] Giono. And Marx, and [Friedrich Engel's] *Anti-Dühring*. The two last two, like children, eat mud, I don't know why. To return to the earth. Actuality. The present. I eat a lot of Marx mud. It's indigestible. So back to [Balzac's] *Seraphita*, Swedenborg, and Durrell, POETRY. We miss you. I think often of Nancy's eloquent silences, Nancy talking with her eyes, her fingers, her hair, her cheeks, a wonderful gift. Music again.

Tuesday morning: just ran over to Henry's and heard you were coming. That makes me immensely happy. When? To Paris? I won't write any more. We'll talk. Love to you both.

Anaïs

[Paris, December 1938]

Larry:

Saw your letter to Villa Seurat and liked it. Funny we used the word "love" at the same moment. I will confess my great weakness, Larry—it's true: criticism breaks me down because, you know, deep down I feel *handicapped*. I feel I am making superhuman efforts to dominate not only a language that is not mine but to say things which I should have said with music and dancing. I am deeply and honestly aware of my faults, I *feel* like a stutterer at times. Worst of all, I suffer because when I look at the bad phrase I can't see it as bad. Imagine a painter being color blind. Yes, at a certain moment I shake my head as a Chinaman would and say: What's the matter with "belly-well"; why can't I say "belly-well" instead of "very well"? I can't say "very well." I know you want to protect me from ridicule. I should not get desperate. But I feel differently now. As soon as I'm sure again of the faith and love then I feel equal to this struggle in the dark which is different from the English writer's struggle. Mine is not laziness or neglect but certain tone-deaf moments. I will let you help me. I got over the neurotic feeling of being ridiculous, etc.

Soon.

Sorry if the female showed undue defense-poisons. I didn't *bite*, did I?

I'm dedicating the book to you and Nancy. Now will you tell Nancy this: Kahane says white [for the cover] is impossible. Shops won't take it. Ask her if she can make another suggestion for the cover. She's the painter in the family. Ask her if all grey with white letters would be all right, or black with all-over design in white ink of magnified snow drops, dropped carelessly?

Love,

Anaïs

2 Rue Cassini, Paris 14me [December 1938]

Dear Larry:

Sorry I failed to appear that afternoon. Everybody decided to call on me just as I was leaving, the men with the telephone, the moving men, the Prefecture with a note saying [my] briefcase has been found, etc., etc. I couldn't move. And at 4 I thought you'd be gone already.

If I remember, you said you didn't want to see Eduardo.[62] In that case would you write in one of the *Black Book*s and mail it to him with a disguised handwriting? I promised him he would get a copy. I didn't say you were in London. The other copy is for Thurema Sokol. Please write in it. She is the monster, but absolutely *unaware* of it, innocent one, you know what I mean.

[...]

[Anaïs]

[Paris, December 1938]

Dear Larry, who doesn't write me:

Eduardo says to tell you [W.H.] Auden was born Feb. 21 (like Anaïs), [Stephen] Spender Feb. 28, [George] Barker February 26—and you, I believe, the 25th![63] We should have a Pisces banquet someday.

Where are you that you don't write me? Eduardo is awaiting *The Black Book* as a Christmas present. Please mail it with disguised writing, unless you see him.

Hugo and I saw *The Black Book* at the window of the Rue de Rivoli book shop—very much in sight. We stood and gloated over it, commenting on the charms and values of Lawrence Durrell.

---

[62] Eduardo Sánchez (1904-1990) was A.N.'s beloved cousin who inspired her to undergo psychoanalysis in the 1930s and encouraged her early writing.

[63] L.D. was born February 27, 1912.

Henry sounds happy.[64]

We've just been in [a] Chinese trance—my place fixed like A Thousand and One Nights—like a hypnotic. We don't go out. Music, incense, dreaming, writing.

Hugo is returning the 3rd which doesn't mean you have to move out, you know that.

Love to you both,
Anaïs

[Paris, December 1938]

Dear Larry:

Will you please forward this letter to my Father. I made believe I was in London so as to elude all family festive (?) gatherings during the holidays. To rest from all connections. And give the other letter to Henry. Don't mix them up! Waiting to hear your plans.

Love to you both,
Anaïs

[Paris, December 1938]

Dear Larry:

Do me a big big big BIG BIG BIG BIG BIG BIG BIG BIG BIG favor: Edward O'Brien of *The Best Short Stories* has written me a note asking for biographical details. I suppose this means he is including the "Birth" piece in the collection as the note is sent care of Dorothy

---

[64] At the instigation and with the support of the Durrells, H.M. had gone to London for a brief visit over the Christmas holidays. (*AIJ5*, p. 94)

Norman.[65] Now I'm stupid about writing about myself and I like that piece you did down in Corfu. Please be good enough to make a copy of it (H.M. tells me he returned it to you or I would have made a copy) and send it directly to Edward O'Brien [in] London as soon as possible. He asked me to hurry. If you get inspired you might finish off with a little about the FEROCIOUS temperament. But if not, it is good as it is. H.M. liked it.

The megaphone ME ME ME ME underlined that you kidded me about me not ME but in the mouth of June, alias Alraune, alias Johanna.[66]

We had a quiet Christmas at home. And you? I would have called you up midnight but I was sure you were out on a gay night, and I hated calling up finding you were out, and maybe sort of collectively jealous. Love to all,

Anaïs

[P.S.] Hugo is returning to London Jan. 3. Please forward Hugo's mail. Telephone Odeon 51-45.

12 Rue Cassini, Paris 14me [January 1939]

Dear Larry:

As we haven't heard from you we're imagining you're staying in London—so I'm sending you with Hugo part 3 of the novel, the carbon of what I gave Kahane, as while he reads the M.S. you have time to mark up this one—right on the M.S.—whatever corrections you think

---

[65] "Birth" was published in *The Best Short Stories of 1939* (Houghton Mifflin, 1939).

[66] Various names for one of the key characters in "Djuna," based on H.M.'s second wife, June Miller.

necessary.[67] Kahane said I was handing it in too late for Feb. 21.

The other two parts I can't send because of Hugo and you know them by heart—so send me your notes on them, will you—the Hans, Johanna, Father part. You will see I separated them completely and they hang together better than when I tried to weave them together. Thus part three takes up all the themes in one.

Larry, listen, I know you got the impression that I'm *touchy* about criticism. Please try to understand I went through a long grind with H.M. over every word, and I was simply discouraged to see there was still something the matter, that's all. I don't know why I'm writing you anyway—I have a feeling everything is wrong this time between us. The New Year was dismal—among the things which depressed me was the mental note I made: everything askew with Larry. Because you didn't read the M.S. when you had time, didn't send the notes and haven't written. Have I sinned somewhere?

Love,

Anaïs

[P.S.] Give these to Henry, please, and tear up my letters if you're staying with Hugo.

12 Rue Cassini, Paris 14me [January 1939]

Dear Nancy and Larry:

Was pleased with your letter announcing another TWIN SOUL! I'm coming to look at it. Meanwhile,

---

[67] "The Voice" was the third novella included in *The Winter of Artifice*.

Goetfried [H.M.] and I have sweated over the proofs [of *The Winter of Artifice*] and made many improvements for which I want to pay the expenses. I am taking the proofs to Kahane before I leave for London, hoping by that time to have received Larry's version, which I will confront with my set, and tell him to charge expense of correction to you, but I will settle with you for it as it is not fair. All this has come about through all your struggles, and I now see what a lot of lousy writing I did, and I am really sorry. But it is really very much improved now; Goetfried let nothing pass. We used a magnifying glass, and [with] Larry's corrections it should be all right now. I am waiting for Larry's set very keenly. Then I take it to Kahane and come to London in a holiday mood, light and ready to play. If l can, I will bring you a dummy for your approval.

Goetfried is obsessed now with *Seraphita*, writing about her.[68] And preparing for Capricorn Two.[69]

Love to both of you,

Anaïs

---

[68] H.M.'s essay, "*Seraphita*," first appeared in Paris in *Volontes* (#16, April 1939, Part 1; #17, May 1939, Part 2) and in London in *The Modern Mystic* (May, 1939) and was eventually included in the volume *The Wisdom of the Heart* (Norfolk, Connecticut: New Directions, November 1941. (*AIJ5*, p. 96)

[69] Most likely the beginnings of what would be the *Rosy Crucifixion* novels.

12 Rue Cassini, Paris 14me [February 1939]

Dear Larry:

Trying to fix *Winter of A.* Send me the notes you made so I can work over them, please. Hope [no one will] intrude so you can enjoy the place [H.G.'s London apartment]. How do you like the aquarium up in the ceiling? Wanted to talk to you before you left. Felt you were in trouble—somehow—but you sort of laugh at my "psychologizing" so I was afraid. You must come back to Paris when you can get into Villa Seurat. I'll be alone then, not going to fancy movies on [the Champs] Elysées or anything.

Don't Flutter So Blindly, Larry.

Georgette Leblanc, who lived with [Maurice] Maeterlinck, said they lived in *"la forêt du majuscule"*— the forest of capital letters.

Notice *modern* typing does away with them. Why, doctor Durrell?

How much do I owe you for the *Black Books*? The other two I would like here to give away at Xmas. If you need those 2 in London I can get them from Kahane. Shall I?

Love to you and Nancy,
Anaïs

12 Rue Cassini, Paris 14 [March 1939]

Dear Larry:

I kept postponing an answer to your lovely watery green birthday letter. (I tell you, you're the only one whose letters seem like little gems fallen out accidentally from the very mosaic of your work.) I thought I would be coming over [to London] in person. I still hope so—

perhaps next Thursday. I've been absolutely knocked out physically. A new pose! *Tubéreuse aux muqueuses pleureuses!*[70]

This new "act," as you might call it, requiring me to stay much at home, lying about, perhaps necessary to a crystallization about writing, etc. Need of inner peace. So I started the book on the *Péniche* to amuse myself, a real fairytale—a modern Odyssey—only with shadows (tried to read the first *Odyssey* but it was too much daylight).

And how is your Odyssey going? A wonderful feat of atmospheric enchantment—climate—light. (This reminds me of the low-down whore whose slightly literary man wants to leave her. She suggests they try living in a new country. He retorts it's her *atmosphere* he's tired of. She goes into tantrums because she says she's been called everything but never an "atmosphere," and that's the limit, she won't take that from any man!)

But what I liked was the "Hamlet" poem—the best as poem yet—very pure and rich. I didn't dare keep the copy; thought I had to return it. I wanted to show it to Goetlieb. Send it to him.[71]

Glad to see the poems I knew in *Seven*. It seems to me Durrell the poet is loudly recognized and admired in England, no?

It's been the Poem year for you. I'm glad. I think the "Hamlet" is really perfect, a culmination.

---

[70] Literally meaning "tuberose with mourning mucous membranes," this was the title of one of A.N.'s 1935 diary volumes.

[71] A.N. is probably referring to L.D.'s "The Sonnet of Hamlet," which appeared in the poetry issue of *Delta* (Easter 1939), the last issue of the successor to *The Booster*. (*AIJ5*, p. 97)

You bring up the point of thought or sensation very well. It's here you and I have been tearing each other's hair, your nice gold one and my slightly dyed one!

Henry Miller on the island of Hydra, Greece, 1939.

I seem to be going deeper into writing as sensation—bathing in it uncritically as you do at a concert, seeking to be led only by the instinct, the pleasure in the flesh of words, the voluptuousness. You say: not integrated images. True of surrealism. But not true of your purely sensory pages in *The Black Book*—[an] absolute series of sensory descriptions, in this and in the Carols you followed all the wildest detours of your imagination and your extremely emotional, feeling self (excuse me). Now I do believe all this has to be held together by *meaning* or a thought. I don't like surrealism because it has no orientation, theme or core. It is chaos.

What is arbitrary is *which* meaning: this we can discuss forever. I can say that some of the pages in *The Black Book* that seem the wildest to me represent a marvelously successful attempt to give the prolongation of the sexual experience, its flowerings into a million mystical flowers, its intensification of sensibilities, like a drug. Somewhere you get out of an automobile and lie in a field with a woman. *Très bien*. The writing breaks completely away from its reflective, analytical rhythm into a dance, a swift multiplication of sensibilities, a *fever*. It's sensation. Sensation overflows from its vase, and seems not integrated. But read Dostoevsky and it will give you the same feeling.

I feel that you are so lyrical, so emotional deep down that you are right in seeking a form to rule all this ocean. And being masculine you seek this form as a container, a frame—for this even the form of the poem. You seek the intellectual control. Fine. It's your way. But inside you there is a runaway horse of sensation.

I cannot organize your way. I find that by yielding like the mystic, being receptive, passive, etc., accepting the ocean, seeking no objectivity, I find that I get *there* by *feeling*. My thoughts never lead me anywhere. In music, you see, my ideal is Debussy, not Bach. I don't like to see the construction. I like [Debussy's] *La cathédrale engloutie*. My sensations or feelings have led me to a world that is not a chaos at all, but in which every word is significant. If there is a chaos apparent it's due to bad writing, bad technique, but not to the orientation by the third eye!

Remember—I used to be led by an Idea. Nothing fecund came of it. A book on Lawrence. As soon as I began to swim in the Neptunian current, the Tibetan flow, too—it was fecund.

Any time you wish I can give you a clear intellectual summary of the meaning of *The Winter of Artifice*, and even of *The House of Incest*.

Sensation makes you find the symbol, the sensual image, but underneath it is guided by a vision, a sense. It isn't blind. The blind sensation seekers take drugs or alcohol, and shipwreck at café tables. Does this make any sense?

Well, if I don't see you soon you'll have to buy a yawl (ouch, I can't spell it yet) and visit us on the Riviera.

Love to you and Nancy,

Anaïs

Shortly after Nin's letter to Durrell, Miller left France for Greece, where he spent time with the Durrells; World War II broke out; Jack Kahane died; Nin and Guiler fled to New York. These events scattered the "three musketeers," and Nin's correspondence with Durrell practically ended.

We have only fragments of Durrell's letters to Anaïs Nin from Athens (held in the University of California Los Angeles), describing his work in the British Embassy, his entry-point into the British information service in which he would work intermittently for the next fifteen years.

[Athens]

Anais dear: it is so long since I have written to you that it is beyond all apology; and not because I had nothing to write, or no time to write in, but simply because events moved either too fast or too slow, the necessary tempo wasn't there. It seems for the last month I am walking about the big white rooms over the sea, watching the gulls, and beginning to write letters to you which never end. Now in this damned hotel where the trams screech all night I metamorphose them into the sound of the lift at rue Gazan, with ice on the pond, and the swans at anchor, and your particular kind of soft ring on the doorbell. I wanted really to write from the peace of tea-time on our own balcony at Corfu; that would have been an intelligible way of approaching you. At tea-time the tall shadows from the cypress meet the sea; ultramarine crashes down through fierce blue chords to green and gold. Albania opens into huge dark fissures, and becomes strangely Tibet. Tea, honey, silence. The water lapping at the edges of one's heart.

The first moonlight entry into the bottleneck harbour of the Bay of Fauns; autumn with the first thrust of asphodel on the bare tumulus of rock. The lift and kick of the inexpert *Van Norden* [72] the day the squall came up and nearly took us down. Or the wild northern cove where we landed dazed one day to the tune of the cicada and shared the beach with the herringgulls, mending our oars and not speaking. In my imagination I am always thinking and loving those bare tumps of rock to the north

---

[72] The Durrells' boat in Corfu, named after a character in *Tropic of Cancer*.

where the sea thrashes and uncoils all the year long, and where no vegetation can grow except the green spiny cactus. It is a kind of internal catechism of places: the places I have touched there. The scented bay where we landed one morning on our way round; clarid, still, icy, with a thick shock of coloured weed visible in two fathoms. To switch off the engine and glide to anchor is like a spiritual entering of silence. A red house and an avenue of cypresses to the water's edge. In the soft spring mist an English cuckoo with an Ionian voice. And a man singing "Monaxia" somewhere out of sight; Loneliness, Loneliness. Even in sagging demotic jazz the Grecian bareness was poetic.

He refers lovingly to Corfu:

[...] the immense circularity of the sea, the way the waters were pushed up to our feet, to taste our toes like warm grapes on some beach where perhaps no men have ever been, but only natural birds without fear and shame, without anguish and psychology. I would trade the remotest caravan routes of Asia for a Dukedom of Kouloura in Corfu, if it were only the rock with the house of white rock built upon it. If it were only the six foot margin the law allows to freebooters on the sea-line. The islands are in my blood, the bare beauties.

[In Athens,] our day is pleasantly enough spent typing and yawning and typing but a life of dissipation spiritually. I am not used to living with three noisy typewriters and a bunch of pleasant humourists. Now that the white lice have cut the wires to the brain and pitched us into the war everything takes place in a soft unreal way, like the submerged cathedral; labyrinthine routines; long corridors of paper and memoranda. The conception of war is like some long slowly palpitating track of viscera opening to engulf us; no end visible. Only the multiplication of imbecilities to ten places of decimals. In a deep sense this is Hugo's war; it is a banker's war.

[New York, first half of 1946]

Dear Larry:

I wanted to write you for a long time—never forgot you. Love the "Carol" particularly[73]—but my life has been a chaos since I came here or I might say a desert—break with Henry followed by small relationships, all bastard ones, work to print, etc. I won't go into that.[74] A friend of mine, Kimon Friar, will bring you this letter.[75] He will give you the better aspect of my activities. He is an interesting and vital person.

Write me. I hear you are printing too. Have you anything to send me here that I can show my publisher? He is Gore Vidal of [E.P.] Dutton, a friend, a boy of 20 whose first novel is appearing June 15.

---

[73] L.D.'s *Zero and Asylum in the Snow* was published privately in Rhodes in 1946.

[74] For details of A.N.'s break with H.M. and her subsequent affairs, see *Mirages: The Unexpurgated Diary of Anaïs Nin, 1939-1947*.

[75] Kimon Friar (1911-1993) was a prolific American scholar, poet, critic and translator of modern Greek literature; in the 1940s, he hosted readings in which A.N. participated.

Kimon needs no description: he is one of the very few articulate human beings in the U.S.A. He made me read and lecture for the first time. He is a poet.

Send me any MS you have. And poems for *Voices*.[76] Will write you soon.

Love,
Anaïs

[New York, mid-1946]

Dear Larry:

Kimon sent me your letter. It was also the long interval between our communications which blocked me into silence, although I too thought often about you, heard about you, read your poetry which I like if you don't, discussed you with my friends, so that they all read you, know you.

A friend of mine, Claude Frederick, who has a Press, is writing you—wants to print more poems.[77] At the place of one of the best of the younger poets here, James Merrill, I was handed (at Amherst College) your last book of poems[78] which we read aloud. You are always placed among the best. So *voilà*!

---

[76] Most likely *Voices: A Quarterly of Poetry*, edited by Harold Vinal (New York).

[77] A.N. is probably referring to Claude Fredericks (1923-2013), whose Banyan Press published works by important writers, including A.N.'s friend and Pulitzer-Prize-winning poet James Merrill (1926-1995).

[78] Most likely *Cities Plains and People* (Faber, 1946).

I'm mailing you *Ladders to Fire*—my last book out October—my first by a commercial publisher [Dutton]. The one I most wanted you to read, *Under a Glass Bell*, is out of print and I'll have to wait for the English edition (contract signed 2 years ago).

So much has happened. H[enry]'s ego, self-indulgence, desire to live in the sun still under Hugo's protection finally aroused rebellion and caused a break. Then I had a relationship to a Peruvian [Gonzalo More] who was a mixture of Heathcliff and Othello, six or eight years of violence, parasitism, ending in rebellion. Now I live by a constellation of relationships, unable to find the One as improbable as the Absolute. Is there no one with whom I can communicate as human being, woman, womb and imagination too? Evidently not. I'm not bitter.

I write 10 pages a day, which always sift down to one good one. See many people. Have two or three friends close enough—either sensual or mystical. I have met the Rimbaud of America—19 years old—William Burford.[79] When they are subtle they are homosexuals. When they are lusty they are opaque (like Edmund Wilson)...pigs. I have become (this will astonish you) a dramatic reader of my own work—holding 400 spellbound in one auditorium—at Dartmouth College.

You could walk in any day into our one-room studio with painted skylight windows, and feel utterly at home, with Hugo's copper plates[80] all around, diary on a sofa,

---

[79] Burford (1927-2004) was an American poet and early friend of James Merrill with whom A.N. had a brief romantic infatuation.

[80] On which H.G. engraved.

and friends—none aged—a musician, a dancer, a poet, an actor...*de la meilleure qualité*. The Diary reached its 67th volume.

I was enchanted with the "Carol"—always loved that piece. Should have written you then. If you have a story, or a book, send it. I'm in touch with all the publishers, magazines and a man at Harvard who wants to print stories separately in small booklets.

Hugo is greatly changed—out of his snail-shell, a good engraver, delicate, imaginative.

I hope someday to visit you. For the first time I am earning something which may enable me to pay off debts and travel, I pray, hope, long. Such claustrophobia here since the war. A *camp de luxe*—but a desert as far as way-of-living goes. Inhuman, sexless people—awkward, guilt-ridden, race of neurotics, high percentage of insanity—rootless, earthless, wombless, castrates.

Did you ever see the magazine in which my stories appeared in Greek?

Send me a good photograph, Larry. Write me. Have you any copies of your first book published by Obelisk? I'm sure it could be reprinted. Could you get me a copy? It cannot be had here. My copy is in Paris.

Love, *comme toujours*,
Anaïs

PART TWO: THE POST-JUSTINE YEARS

1957-1976

Lawrence Durrell, ca. 1960.

Diary entry, June 1957: This month the most faun-like relationship was with Lawrence Durrell via his book *Justine.* Twenty years ago Larry appeared in Paris, and in the diary he is a small, blond, blue-eyed, soft-gestured, tanned, endless talker-poet, with yogi suppleness of body, and the power later manifested in the mystifying *Black Book* not apparent.

The Black Book (Obelisk Press) was banned and remained known to very few people. He continued to write poetry and to be published in England. Twenty years later Gore [Vidal] mentions *Justine.* A banquet! An orgy of words and colors, riot of the senses. A male counterpart to my novels. Erratic, elusive, penetrating, a sensuous jungle, a trapezoid of images, a juggler, a master of all prestidigitations.

There was an epidemic of Durrell. Hugo read it; Tom Payne[81] and I talked about it.

The image of Larry, as a young man, was so clear. He had a softly-contoured face; he was not lean, in spite of sailing his boat in Greece. He had a rounded nose, humorous and earthy, comfortable. He passed certain judgments on Henry.

An absurd accident had cut the thread between us. It was he [*sic*] who had paid for the publication of *The Winter of Artifice, Black Spring* [*sic*] and *The Black Book.*[82] During the war he found himself needing money. He wrote to Henry. It was at the time when I was drowning

---

[81] Editor-in-chief of Avon Books, whose specialty was mass market reprints of classic novels.

[82] It was Nancy Durrell who financed the three Villa Seurat Series books.

in debts. I could not help. Henry borrowed from friends. I felt so guilty. The guilt paralyzed me. We could have been writing to each other. I would have followed his life. Of the three of us, he was the best writer. (Unpublished diary)

[Los Angeles, October 1957]

Dear Larry:

The advent of *Justine* was a phenomenon, after the miserly, sterile, frigid, plain, homely, prosaic, stuttering world of American writing. It was truly a fiesta, and a banquet, an orgy. As soon as I began reading, the world expanded. It was not only the great tactile richness, the colors, the smells, the flavors of the surfaces, the atmosphere, but the sudden depths of insight, the senses and the intelligence both so keen. I was tempted to say *this is not writing but witchcraft*. Whatever it is, dear Larry, I must tell you I have an immense respect for what you have done.

All these years, what you amassed in power and color! I went back immediately and reread *The Black Book*. The richness of writing was there, and the deftness of characters, but more abstract, more mystifying, more distilled. Here the balance is perfect, in *Justine*, between the realism and the surrealism. Surface and depth. The interweaving and the interacting between various levels of consciousness, perfectly captured. The wavering boundaries between dreaming and feeling. The person-ages live vividly for the moment you grasp them, and then disappear again into the depths, and reappear into a flow of poetry. The poetry with which the city becomes the bodies, and the bodies a city. All the metamorphosis of mind and matter, senses and thought. Such imagery: Yes, I know this may sound extravagant, but the writing was extravagantly beautiful. I won't say more so you will believe me. It was strange how it resuscitated the young Larry of twenty-six or so who appeared in Paris and into the pages of the journal and with whom I should have then and there run away with. Because from that day on, in the particular world I was going to traverse artistically, I was to be completely alone. As you well know, with Henry it was the contraries, not parallelism of any kind. Anyway, I can now read *Justine*.

What are you doing in France?[83] How are you living? I am mailing you my books today. You re-entered the flow of the diary (a mighty river now) to have your portrait added to. I live a divided life. One in New York with Hugo-the-father, a graceful apartment, chic clothes, white heat living, many friends, café life in the Village, trips to Mexico, business, and another life here with Rupert-the-son, grandson of Frank Lloyd Wright, nature man, beach man, and professor by mistake, by temperament a guitar player hating work.[84] We wear sloppy clothes, rush off to the beach whenever possible, dream of a catamaran, of surfboarding, have friends, but they are colorless because California is colorless, like a cheap drug that has been mixed with bicarbonate and tooth-

---

[83] L.D. rented a house called Villa Louis in Sommières.

[84] By this time, A.N. had entered into a bigamous marriage with Pole.

paste, a pseudo-tranquilizer. And I Just finished a novelette on Mexico, on a mythical city called Golconda.[85]

Is there anything you want from America? If you ever come we can put you up in New York. Are there any books you want? Anything in fact?

Do write me.

I have bought many copies of *Justine* and am giving it to friends.

I have sent a copy to Sweden where I was beautifully translated and where I am a best seller. I have given *Justine* to my pocketbook editor (25 cent editions) who published my last one.

Gore Vidal, a friend, who wrote on your jacket, first mentioned *Justine* to me. He admires it deeply.

Devotedly,

Anaïs

Letter from Anaïs Nin to Rupert Pole:
[New York, November 1957]

My love,

Situation at Avon chaotic and critical for Thomas Payne. The owner died in Hollywood of being forced to drink with a bleeding ulcer.

But—he was so enthusiastic about my reprint of *Under a Glass Bell*, its appearance, my cutting through red tape, obstacles, commercial wholesale quantities, etc. that he is taking care of distribution of *any book I do*. He

---

[85] Originally titled *Solar Barque* and privately published in 1958, the novel was expanded and republished as *Seduction of the Minotaur* in 1961.

said: how exciting and wonderful to be doing a book one loves after doing all day books one despises! His help is free and very valuable. So I will do Durrell's *Black Book*, which is [now] selling for $45 a copy—and Payne will take 2,000 [copies] and I'm in business—even after paying the writer I can make money.

Cost of reprinting Durrell: $400

Distributor pays $0.40 a copy on 2,000: $800

Mailing list has bought 150 *Bells* to date, so suppose they buy 150 Durrells: $150

Conservative earning estimate is $1,000—of which I can give Durrell whatever is fair.

Payne says I'm very practical. But oh, the work! Correspondence to *start*. Afterwards all I have to do is deliver the books to the distributor (all *big* paperback shops) with a mailing list.

Anaïs

[New York, November 1957]

Dear Larry and Claude:[86]

When people telephone me: "Anaïs, my husband left me, what shall I do?" I say: read *Justine*. When they say: "Anaïs, my novel was rejected and I feel suicidal," I say: read *Justine*. When they say: "I want to go to Paris and I can't, I have no money, help me," I say: read *Justine*. It is an epidemic...a Durrell epidemic. Last night we talked about you with a close friend, Thomas Payne, the very intelligent editor-in-chief of Avon (who published *Spy* in

---

[86] L.D. met Claude-Marie Vincendon in Cyprus in 1955 and began living with her in 1956; they married in 1961.

the $.25 books). He reads tons, for his job, and for his own personal taste. I made him read *Justine*. He had not loved a book as much for years and years. He was probing about for possibilities of a reprint in a cheap edition (even without blessings from the publisher). It seems (unofficially) that Dutton is not pushing the reprint, reserving your book for possible inclusion in their own pocket classics...but this is unofficial so use it obliquely...

Now I have a project. After sitting and waiting for three years for my out-of-print books to be reprinted (*Spy* was taken only because of the salability of the title) I got impatient and offset *Under a Glass Bell* (the one I sent you). It sells for one dollar. It is going so well that I began to dream of offsetting your *Black Book*. Has it ever been reprinted? Thomas Payne thought it would be a wonderful idea. My scheme is this: non-profit except for the writer. It would cost about 50 cents to offset the original (like photography) with an interesting cover (either an engraving by Hugo or some terrific super-imposition photograph done by a friend (I would mail you suggestions). It would sell for one dollar. You would get all that comes back after paying printing (I will pay that out of what is coming back from *Under a Glass Bell*). When we sell directly (I have a mailing list from the Press, and from having had to take care of my own books all these years), this would eliminate the problem of censorship (no reviews). A kind of underground activity.[87]

Hugo is finishing a film for the Brussels Film Festival.
Anaïs

---

[87] The short-lived private Anaïs Nin Press was a way for A.N. to get her work in print in lieu of commercial publishers.

Diary entry, Los Angeles, December 1957: I said playfully [to Thomas Payne]: "Be my partner in publishing for pleasure only!" He said: "What a relief to publish freely after working all day to push books I don't like." He was enthusiastic about the *Black Book*—until Larry Durrell put an end to the project.[88]

Los Angeles, February 18, 1958

Dear Larry:

How pleased and interested I was by your letter in which you answered some of my questions about your work. How wise you were in knowing the dangers of being swallowed by [keeping] a diary. I am still con-founded by the richness of the material I have not been able to transpose. I wrote about *Justine* for a woman's magazine, but they did not have space enough to do it justice. On this end of the trapeze, I have been working on an article on Caresse Crosby[89] and Citizens of the World in Delphi, a wonderful story...also going through a fabulous experiment similar to Aldous Huxley's *The Doors of Perception*. Did you read the book? LSD is a refinement of mescaline, the Mexican mush-room, and

---

[88] E.P. Dutton had contracted *The Black Book* and published it in 1960.

[89] Caresse Crosby (1891-1970), an American friend and confidante of A.N., ran the Black Sun Press with her husband Harry Crosby and published several expatriot writers in France during the 1930s.

possibly the Hindu soma. It gives visions, hallucinations, and makes you dream in such a concentrated, heightened fashion, telescoped and time-less. But for me it was merely a proof that the world of the artist, the world of the unconscious, are one, and some can only reach it by chemicals, but the artist already has access to it, as do the analysts... That was all I wanted to know. I will send you a copy of the voyage I took (twelve hours) soon. Huxley has an extended knowledge of this lore, and we had endless discussions because he says it is new; I say it is familiar and recognizeable, as dreaming is.

Yes, of course we will take a detour to visit you, any detour. And we will not give away your address. I know what it is.

Hugo is working feverishly on perfecting his film.[90]

Here is a photo of Rupert Pole, so you can become acquainted with him. He is of Welsh origin, sings and plays the guitar, plays the viola, his father was a famous Shakespearean actor (Cambridge), and his stepfather is the son of Frank Lloyd Wright, the architect. Rupert's obsession is to build a house. He will this summer, by the sea. But Los Angeles is in the middle of nowhere. Have you read Nathaniel West's *Day of the Locust* or *Miss Lonelyhearts*? Los Angeles *est le néant*. But Rupert is non-uprootable.

---

[90] H.G., a self-taught engraver, became interested in making experimental films at the beginning of the 1950s and went on to be a well-respected filmmaker whose films are collected in the Museum of Modern Art in New York and the Cinématique Française in Paris. His *nom d'artiste* was Ian Hugo.

I look out to a small patio filled with semi-tropical plants. The dog is chewing up a bone. Rupert is about to come home from the school where he teaches and the children are giving him a birthday party today. (February!) Then we will have a gin and tonic while I cook dinner. And we will see Romain Gary, author of *Racines aux ciel* (did you read that?) and his wife Lesley Blanch (*Wilder Shores of Love*)—do you know her? Romain is a super-neurotic, which is an achievement in the diplomatic service, and Lesley doesn't care whether she ties her picnic basket with an old pencil. Hollywood is baffled at such a French consul!

Devotedly,
Anaïs

[New York, early 1958]

Larry:

Now I am sipping *Justine* like a rare liqueur, loving every word. So rich in meaning it yields and yields.

Message from Themistocles Hoetis[91] that he was given *Bitter Lemons* to review for *The New York Times* and will do your *Justine* (he is editor of *Zero*, author of *The Man Who Went Away*). Knowing you are working so hard, I don't want to write long letters. We'll talk in May. Can I read Claude's books?[92] Are you in touch with Olympia Press? Can they be trusted?

---

[91] George Solomos, a.k.a. Themistocles Hoetis, was an American writer and editor of *Zero: Anthology of Literature and Art.*

[92] Claude's titles include *Mrs. O'* (1957); *The Rum Go* (1958); and *A Chair for the Prophet* (1959); published by Faber & Faber.

Love,
Anaïs

[New York, early 1958]

Dear Larry:

I do understand about Dutton and *The Black Book*. Bear in mind that *if* they should not publish it within the promised time I will still be ready to do it...

I read *Bitter Lemons* with enjoyment—first of all to catch up with your life and then for the delight I take in your writing. I see two Lawrences—one conscious and objective, the other unconscious and internal (*Justine*).

I liked all you wrote me about my books except the word "deliberate." Nothing was ever more of a blind labyrinth than this association of images made without knowledge of its directions of geography—mathematics in the dark. A deliberate book (or books) would have been so easy to write. I wanted to ask you about the diary. I find in mine that once long ago you thought it a dangerous journey into the labyrinth, and you pleaded that I should surface. Did you have one of your own then, secret, or later? Is the fragmentation of diaries in *Justine* a proliferation of yours? Mine did help me to maintain a center of radiations.

I continue to work for your renown and recognition. Be glad it did not come sooner. Fifteen years ago America was not ready: it would have given you an acid reaction. I was published, but I feel and know now it was too soon. I got the full brunt, malice of the so-called realists, the social critics, the anti-poetic, the anti-unconscious, anti-symbol, etc. Today it has changed. Even the journalists admit symbolism in their daily columns.

The lovely smoky quality of *Justine* would have been torn for explicitness, for facts. The waiting must have been painful, I know, and I wish I had known about it, for then I had my own hand-press and we would have published you. But the good timing (after the war, exchange of literature, influence from other countries, the final break with folklore, dislike of anything beyond folklore, plain, homely, peasant prose) will make it up to you.

[Hugo and I] will go to Brussels for the Film Festival in April, then Paris. We must see you. I want to meet Claude. Where will you be? Will you come to Paris? Let me know. More soon...

Love,

Anaïs

[New York, March 1958]

Dear Larry:

You didn't say *which* month, but any day in May is perfect. We will be in Brussels April 19 to end of April— and May 1 in Paris. May 15th will be perfect. I do hope you meant May. But in any case Hugo and I would like to invite you as guests for a few days. Let us know. If the 15th is the best...and what hotel will you stay at? We might stay at the same one.

I finally got a copy of *Zero* [*and Asylum in the Snow*]. If it should please you to have it in print I will do it, as soon as you say OK. Tell me about Dutton and *The Black*

Book and how did you get on. I see *Bitter Lemons* is getting good reviews.

Will write more later.

Found a marvelous description of you, a truly wonderful portrait of you in [the] Diary I'm copying and editing now—written after you asked me: "You won't write about me in [the] diary?" And I answered: "Of course not!"

Love to you and Claude,

Anaïs

[New York, Spring 1958]

Dear Larry and Claude:

In Brussels c/o Baroness Lambert rue Piedmont April 19 to 25; after: Paris, Hotel Crillon, Place Vendôme [*sic*; actually Place de la Concorde]. If we invite you can you come to Paris during first two weeks of May? For a few days? If not I will travel to you between May 1 and 15—as after that we have to hop around for the business which pays for the trip. If you have beds we will invite you for breakfast, lunch and dinner. Otherwise I will fly to you for a few days. Bringing you a copy of *Zero* [*Anthology of Literature and Art*] to look at.[93]

Love to you both,

Anaïs

---

[93] A.N. contributed to the magazine and encouraged L.D. to, but he never did.

[Paris, Spring 1958]

Dear Larry:

Arrived this morning to find your card. *Hélas*, I have to wait for my brother's arrival May 5 and be here for his concert May 10—after that I can leave—alone. Hugh is here on a business trip paid by his firm and has a million duties—cannot escape.

What a bombardment of all spiritual and emotional atoms to return here after 18 years! I'm quite shattered.

Read *Balthazar* every night. What a magic book. What a prodigious way of encircling all the relativities of truth. An invention of mobility of vision—*la mystique de l'égalité*. You have done it. *Le roman de notre époque*.

I'm sad I can't come immediately—as the "talking" has begun and I hate writing—just now.

Anaïs

[Paris, Spring 1958]

Larry:

Do you want *Lolita* by Vladimir Nabokov, erotica eroticus, Olympia Press.

The trip to Paris would be worth making to see the Peking Opera. Last night an incredible spectacle, Larry— mixture of ballet, aerobatics, painting, dream and defying all laws of gravity—like some of the pages of *Balthazar*— smoke, mystery, sensuous evocations.

Last night reread pages on the desert visit—the brothers announcing marriage to Justine. When did you become a painter as well as a magician?

A

[Paris, Spring 1958]

Dear Larry:

Last night returning from a bistro, a walk, a marionette show, an astrologic banquet, etc. I made a wish that you and Claude could come and share this mescaline fever of rediscovering Paris and this morning your letter came! Wish granted.

No matter how beautiful Gard[94] is the important thing was to talk with you—but preferably here as I was starved for Paris—absolutely suffering from malnutrition of the intelligence and to have you both and Paris is perfection.

You have forgotten the Anaïs who lived in a bathless houseboat. We do not always live like this, only at the Company's expense! I will find you a hotel *with bath* nearby—for the 10th.

I can't feel anything but anger with little Joe. He made a *shabby* and *false* caricature of my 10-year relationship with Henry![95] If I could bring out diary it would explode his book into bits of trash! I can never forgive him for the cheapness and the lie—nor Henry for permitting it!

Much to tell you about *Balthazar* and *Justine*.

My love to you both,

Anaïs

---

[94] Department of France where L.D. lived.

[95] A reference to Alfred ("little Joe") Perlès's book *My Friend Henry Miller* (1955).

[Paris, Spring 1958]

Dear Larry:

We want to do whatever is best for you and your work. If it is better for you I will fly to Marseilles. If you and Claude want to come to Paris, I want to invite you, trip and all. Can we telephone you when we arrive and telegraph friends if necessary? Send us word at the Crillon Sunday.

You can't imagine my pleasure of receiving *Balthazar* the day before I left. I discarded all my other books knowing I could travel thousands of miles with *Balthazar*. I read it every night. It *is again a feast for the intelligence, for the senses, for the heart. Justine* is here in this enchanted house of a most discerning woman, in the aristocratic library—and everyone is reading it.

So much to tell you and so much I want to hear.

Anaïs

[Paris, Spring 1958]

Dear Larry:

I understand—but then I'll have to come down the 11th as I have to return on the 15th. I would have driven down with friends but have to wait for my brother—the 5th to the 10th he'll be here. We had planned a giant bathroom and all kinds of little places to go to—and wanted to share with you a beautiful Paris—warm, sunny, in blossom—and *Lolita* by Nabokov and Ionesco plays at [Théâtre de] la Huchette and Michaux[96] and—

---

[96] Henri Michaux (1899-1984), a Belgian-born poet and writer whom A.N. admired and about whom L.D. wrote.

will it be convenient if I come the 11th? Is it cold? Shall I bring warm clothes—I have them.

Taxi driver told me to read [Paul] Claudel. The delight of [the] discovery I could be in love with a city I thought I had grown frigid to in the U.S.A. We walk walk walk—amorously—over every cobblestone of both past and present superimposed—à la *Balthazar*, Durrell method, multidimensional of fluctuating reality.

Love,

A

[Paris, Spring 1958]

Dear Larry:

As I have to leave May 15, will it suit you if I come down after Joaquín's concert Saturday night the 10th?

I wish you could see Peking Opera. When will you be down? Be sure not to miss it. Still in state of euphoria.

Saw [Ossip] Zadkine and [Stanley] Hayter, and bought books, and even attending the defunct Cirque Medrano did not puncture the magic city.

No interviewer turned up—but who should I see for my books to be translated into French? This I would love above all else. We will begin to come oftener.

Incidentally Hugo is HUGH GUILER, not Guyler.

If you had come you would have seen his 4 films at Cinématique Française, and such restaurants we have unearthed for you!

Any change of plans? Have you a phone?

Love,

Anaïs

[Paris, Spring 1958]

Dear Claude and Larry:

I want to thank you for my deepest and loveliest days in Europe, the riches banquet of intimate delights. It was good I came to you, as being taken with your life was a truer and quicker way of finding and knowing you than our frivolous meeting in Paris.

I hope I can come back but not imprisoned by Hugo's official life. I hope you weren't tired. I love you both.

Anaïs

Letter from Anaïs Nin to Rupert Pole:
Paris, May 13, 1958

Darling:

Saturday night, hearing the Durrells could not come [to Paris], I boarded a train and went to Nîmes as there is a Fair and Festival of Midi painters and I could cover my trip and charge.[97] I'm so glad I did. Not only are Durrell and his wife wonderful, he so deep and she so gay, but to see the Arlesienne countryside, the Nîmes Arena, to find again the beauty I had missed so much, the river, the house, the Roman town, the bridges, the castles. The Durrells have a small peasant house, but a lovely garden. They grow all their vegetables. No hot water, no bathroom, no W.C.! It is like Mexico.

---

[97] To keep R.P. from knowing she was traveling with H.G.—whose expense account paid for her trip to Nîmes—A.N. had made up a fictitious magazine job to explain her comings and goings.

You cool bottles by lowering them into the well. He is very poor as they have two sets of children whom other parents take half the time. Both were married before. Claude is more international than I am—Irish [*sic*], French, brought up in Alexandria, in New Zealand, in France—a saucy girl. I did the painting tour and then they took me to an arena where bulls wear tassels on their horns and the men have to remove them for a prize. They try, and they run for their lives and jump the barrier and some bulls jump too. The whole thing is very gay as there is no death. The men do get hurt now and then, but not as seriously as at bullfights. They drink red wine from morning till night, which keeps everyone glowing but never really drunk. Durrell has known so much poverty that he is obsessed with succeeding. He has been compared to Proust already in France.

We explored Nîmes, sat at the cafés, talked non-stop for two days and I returned this morning tired out, but with my spiritual batteries recharged for years to come. I had to see Durrell to complete the *carnet de bal*. No one could be homelier and so humorous. He has an Irish prizefighter face, a thick potato nose, a large head on a small body, shorter than I, and as fat as Joaquín… So there is nothing to threaten any husband! But you and he would hit it off—he hates cities, loves the sea, used to have a boat; they paddle a canoe down the river and swim. As soon as you get out of Paris you can live on nothing.

Love,

A

L.D. and Claude with A.N. at Villa Louis, Sommières, 1958, with L.D.'s daughter Sappho Jane (l) and Claude's children Diana and Barry Forde.

Letter from Anaïs Nin to Henry and Eve Miller:
Los Angeles, May 19, 1958

Dear Henry and Eve:

I thought you would like to hear about my visit to the Durrells. I took a sleeper to Nîmes, and Larry was at the station early that morning and we recognized each other instantly, which shows how little 18 years had changed us. Claude was waiting at the hotel. Claude, younger, and looking Irish rather than French (she has several nationalities), very lovely, laughing already at 7 AM and we started our two day nonstop talk visit. The house is a farmhouse over a hillside looking down the most wonderful Provence landscape, a Roman chateau and a river with a Roman bridge (they are looking for another house). Larry's paintings[98] are very joyous and colorful, pinned all over the walls with his reviews and photographs. Monastic and primitive. A garden with grapevines that Larry kept trimming. Much red wine.

Claude talks more than Larry, excitedly. Larry seems like a wounded person. His body is quiet while Claude does all the moving, but his eyes are so watchful. He can write all kinds of books, as we know already, marvelous ones, or indifferent ones for money. But he cares about his quartet. I had received *Balthazar* just before leaving for Brussels and Paris. We talked endlessly, about the next books, about *Mountolive*, about America, about you both (he played a record of your interview), about Paris. Until his work is finished he is in a way hiding and does not welcome excitement. He said he had had enough traveling and people.

In the evening we drank a bottle of champagne I had brought plus several bottles of red wine and got hysterically gay until we fell asleep and slept around the clock. The next day early in the afternoon we went to Nîmes to do errands, to have dinner in town before I took the train back. We met F.J. Temple,[99] the writer who printed a small booklet given to him by a friend who inherited [Conrad] Moricand's papers. I believe he had

---

[98] L.D. exhibited his paintings under the name Oscar Epfs.

[99] Frédéric-Jacques Temple (b. 1921), French writer and translator.

met you on your last trip to France. Meanwhile, we covered centuries in space. We wondered why you had not stayed in France. Larry loves it and dreams of living between Provence and Paris. And I was deliriously happy and dream of returning there to stay. Larry has that curious Piscean quality of being immersed in experience, in feeling and yet maintaining a wisdom, an intuition of its meaning. Claude is devoted and loyal, doesn't follow all the intricacies but has a gift for saving him from the dangers of the deep.

I had a little visit with Buchet, Durrell's French publisher. And Girodias![100] Girodias I liked better than his father [Jack Kahane]. Aside from that one doubtful bankruptcy, has he been honest with you? My only sadness is not being published in France and not understanding why. I tried to interest Buchet in all the novels done in one volume.

My love to you both—what a visit that would have been if you both had been down at the same time.

Anaïs

Los Angeles, Monday, June 2, 1958

Dear Larry and Claude:

At six o'clock while you are still asleep, I like to take a glass of red wine while I cook dinner to be transported to your little house and remember the talks we had. Larry, was it the red wine or did you really say that while we are looking at *Justine*, while we think we are

---

[100] Maurice Girodias (1919-1990) took over Obelisk Press and then founded Olympia Press in Paris.

discovering *Justine*, it is Larry you will see and know? While we ate the lovely garden salad (Americans love very young girls because their vegetables are so old and tough, suffering from gigantism) did we listen to Henry's opinion of Tolstoy?

Are you in your new house? Send me photographs.

Hugo has written me news I cannot yet believe. Business has developed—he is staying in Europe, and I may get back. It was such a short, mutilated trip. As soon as it is certain I will tell you. He has a film he wants to make with the [Yves] Joly marionettes.[101] Eve's response to my letter about our visit together was beautiful. It seems I made them feel they were there.

Larry, I can't do a bigger book for the moment—only yours. Here is a small advance ($100) which Hugo will send you in francs—and I will do your stories—soon.[102] I have written to UCLA librarian for *Booster*—and to Henry.

I told Buchet you like the *Spy*. I hope you don't mind. How was your party, or did the political situation spoil it?

Lunch with Huxley and a woman doctor who believe lysergic acid and LSD—the one I took—will cure the neurosis of the world. Someday (when Hugo is not making a film and I have more money for publishing) we'll have to do the book we talked about.

While I write you, Hugo returned to New York for 10 days—then to Curaçao, Cuba and Paris again. So it seems

---

[101] Yves Joly (1908-2013) was a French puppeteer known for his minimalist puppets.

[102] The stories may have been "Zero," "Asylum in the Snow," and "The Paper Womb."

as if I were returning this summer duplex life and all. I will let you know, of course. Meanwhile I received the delightful newspaper clippings!

I know you are deep in work so I won't write much. When you have finished the 4 volumes and have nothing to read I will send you volume 54 of diary as there is a lot that concerns you and will interest you.

For the moment à la George Sand I am nursing my delicate-chested R[upert] through bronchitis.

I want to write you in detail about *Balthazar*. One hesitates to expand too much on a work in progress. The questions one might ask are being answered. Hugo kept the book and as soon as I have it again I will comment on individual beauties.

Have you made any new drawings for *Zero*? Are there any corrections in the text you have? I wrote to Gore about the film, and to my intelligence service in N.Y. secret [info?] on *Justine*.

I sent you [...] [Jack] Kerouac's book[103] so you will get a flavor of American life.

My love to you and Claude. When is your book coming out in New York?

Anaïs

[Los Angeles, Summer 1958]

Larry:

Returning for July and August. Be prepared for a visit from either side of the medal: H[ugo] or R[upert]!

---

[103] *On the Road.*

Leaving 23. No fixed address. Write to NIN c/o Marguerite Rebois, 8 rue Viroflay, Paris 15.

Hugh says let's go to Greece with the Durrells but did not know about your new house,[104] work and children—and need of peace.

Love,

A

[Paris, Summer 1958]

Dear Claude and Larry:

Jean Fanchette[105] is delicious! So intelligent and so warm and generous. I met him first and we liked each other instantly—agree also on many essentials. I saw him again (short moments stolen from complete immersion in business, Hugo's) and he took me to see the painter (I have forgotten his name) you visited too—the little *sacré famille*, the sad paintings and the humorous drawings of Paris. Then Hugo and I saw Jean again before leaving—Hugo [is off] to Brittany, Lausanne, Frankfurt, etc. and I to London to meet R[upert] and begin one of the most difficult of my trapeze acts. I never think about death but I do sometimes think about falling—and no net under me.

We talked—of course—much about you.

---

[104] L.D. and Claude planned to move to an isolated house called the Mazet Michel, near Sommières.

[105] A friend of Durrell with whom A.N. would collaborate on the bilingual literary journal *Two Cities*; the first issue was dedicated to Durrell.

I'm so glad you had us meet [Fanchette]. He was the most interesting one I met in Paris—and I was in danger of cohabitation with ghosts from the past, the All-Seeing [Jean Cateret] (in the stories) being schizophrenic, others (*Under a Glass Bell*) so frivolous and fashionable.

I don't know my plans from day to day. Feel you have enough (or too many) visitors and need peace to work, etc., but may head south and visit for an hour! Please, if we do, do not mention Hugo—that is all...all I ask...

I'm sad that Perlès is getting another chance of misrepresenting Henry, and the undeserved honor of corresponding with you.[106]

Love,

Anaïs

Diary entry, Los Angeles, September 1958: I have decided Durrell is a brilliant cheat who does not have a deep knowledge of character. It shows in this *Balthazar*; he is a *soi-disant* psychiatrist. He promised relativity of truth, but that lies in acceptance of subjectivity and that means introspection, going inward, and he has not. (Unpublished diary)

[Los Angeles, September 1958]

Dear Larry:

The first time I read *Balthazar* too hurriedly, and in the center of too much turmoil. The last few days I

---

[106] L.D. and Perlès had embarked on a project called *Art and Outrage*, consisting of their correspondence about H.M.'s work; it was published in 1959.

devoted my full attention to it; I lay in bed for hours, reading. I always complained of people's inarticulateness, yet I also felt this strange silence as after hearing good music. You are utterly filled, dazed, and elated, yet you do not say a word. But I want to, as you are so far away, and because a writer needs that. He has to know if it was heard. Yes. I might say that the difficulty of reading *Balthazar* after *Justine* is there. And I think I can explain it. One is drugged by *Justine*; it is an experience with magic, but one is seduced by Justine [the character] and wants revelation, concentration upon her. I think many may feel this. I was a little amazed that it was not all her. But once I knew you were offering a different kind of spice, SHE was not the only one...then I read with freedom and delight. It is dangerous, you know, after having provided an aphrodisiac, to offer a banquet of analysis and search. But you accomplished it. The danger lay in our reluctance, when once taken into intimate relationships, by enlarging the circle and entering a larger world of characters. But now, with care, with openness, I received it all. Admired the same gift of painting of sound, music, images. I have no negative reactions. It is quite wonderful the way the "scenes" appear; it is a city; it is a drama; it is the inside of the person. The sensation that it is being dreamed is there, in spite of the fine realistic details. I liked the variations, the careful exact capturing of diverse personalities in each one. The rich paintings developing into a wise truth. And this admission of endless mystery, endless chaos.

Yes, dear Larry, you are a magician. I salute you. I truly spent several days of magnificence and pleasure. Just when the senses have absorbed all they can, then ideas sparkle, philosophy, psychology, history... I did not say much at the time, and forgive me. I do hope you are receiving your proper praise. I wish I were there to talk it over. To ask you questions. Thought about so many things while reading.

When will we talk again? I gave your three stories to the same photomontage photographer[107] who is illustrating *House of Incest*...to do a cover. I will send you a copy of the cover for your approval.

I could write you a lot more, but reached lowest ebb yet in energy with serious anemia...so forced to rest...to read...but not to sit up and write too long. It is hot. We go to the beach on weekends. R. is again the professor of science. Hugo is still in Europe awaiting the great "coup" of fortune...which never comes.

Wonder what you thought of *Solar Barque*, written two years ago, the essence of many trips to Mexico. No word from Gore Vidal. I will write him tomorrow. Your photograph taken by R. came out very fine and I am having a copy made for you.[108] Are you alone again? Able to work? I will never forget how you incited the eagle to spread his wings. I like America less than ever but am so grateful for the calm and dullness and monotony as I can work.

The effect of Balinese music, that was how *Balthazar* sounded. That's what it is, in a way, twelve-toned. A long time ago I was so concerned with the feeling that poetry had to be restored to analysis of character. *Et voilà*.

---

[107] Val Telberg (1910-1995).

[108] A.N. and R.P. visited L.D. in late July 1958.

I have ordered Claude's book by mail. I live in the desert! I know you have no time for letters. And I should be reading instead of writing but I felt overwhelmed with gratitude and had at least to thank you.

Anaïs

[P.S.] Completely forgot to write you about Marguerite [Rebois], friend and astrologer. I had given her *Justine* and she wanted to visit you. Did she? How is Claude? Has she regained her weight?

[Paris, October 1958]

Dear Claude and Larry:

We were in Brussels when *Mountolive* arrived. As soon as I returned I read it. Dear Larry, it is amazing how you can change your point of view, and write a classic novel around a similar theme, *d'autres yeux, d'autres âmes*. I like particularly the lovemaking of Nessim and Justine, such an interweaving of the physical and ideologycal intercourse, and that of Melissa and Mountolive...wait...Darley (I haven't the book, can't check, but it was such a moving effort at connecting). Now I remember—it was Pursewarden. The relationship of Leila and Mountolive, also beautifully done. Yes, remarkable, the change of insight and atmosphere. It was as if you wanted to expose the mirages of passion first, and the cold lucidity following, on a second dimension.

Anyway, I think you have beautifully achieved what you intended to do. Unconscious instinctual first with only intermittent illuminations, then the analytical, then the outer ring of consciousness. Yes, *magnifique* the drama of the two brothers. It is a mystery how you can shift positions. I sent it quickly to Vidal without re-reading it.

It makes me sad that your work was interrupted, sad all of you were ill.

I sent *Zero* out immediately. But the cover, I haven't found anything appropriate. You know I had *The Paper Womb* offset from *The Booster*.

Yes, I have the same impression of Buchet—timid and with his radar out for the other's opinions—they both talked a lot of Henry's visit and want the diary, not my novels. He is so naïve; he says the novel is finished because *Esprit* published the same old obituary of the novel forgetting how often it has appeared!

It looks like no visit—because Hugo needs me here as the only haven between grinding of business, and in August R[upert] arrives and then perhaps we may drive down.

Today we went to Louveciennes. I didn't want to go in, but Hugo did. It was a cemetery—the house, once beautiful, [is] utterly neglected and falling apart (see portrait of it in *Children of the Albatross*).

Hugo is gambling.[109] If all of it does not collapse (due to political events) I will send you another $100 in August, another in Sept. and so on. His work is so unstable and full of mirages.

I will send you photomontages for *Zero* to see if you like them—done by Val Telberg who is doing those for *House of Incest*.

---

[109] H.G. had a habit of investing his money in ill-fated business schemes.

Went houseboat hunting today for a *pied à l'eau* in Paris...but don't think I will move permanently yet.

Do you need books or just peace to write your own?

Anaïs

[New York, November 1958]

Dear Larry:

If it is not too late—do you remember how strongly I felt you should introduce the Miller anthology? At the time I said you carried more influence than the stuffy critics among the people who count, who read, the newer generations. I discussed this with several people when I returned and they felt the same way. Your prestige as an artist and exceptional writer carries further than a few pompous words. *Enfin*, I hope it is not too late and I can write you more eloquently on the subject.

Meanwhile...

I'm mailing photographs for your approval as suggestions for the cover of *Zero and Asylum in the Snow.*

Also, I signed yesterday a sale of *Children of the Albatross* and *The Four-Chambered Heart* to Peter Owen (who publishes Anna Kavan, Henry Miller, Hesse, etc.). It would make me proud to be [introduced] by you—not a big job or strain or stress away from your work, but a focus from you would help me to face England, a presentation. My having been so misrepresented here has made me practically unknown in Europe. Will you say a little out of your fund of wisdom and clear-sightedness? I ask hesitantly because I know [A] *Spy* [*in the House of Love*] is your favored one—and because you are overworked—yet it means a great deal to me and I hold my breath until you write.

Anaïs

In November 1958, Durrell wrote Nin a card and said: "Of course I'll do you a preface...by when should I send it in? Yes, I've done one for Henry and he seems to like it." (Unpublished diary)

[Los Angeles, November 1958]

Dear Larry:

So happy to get your card just before leaving New York. The day before I had mailed you on a letter from Peter Owen explaining hurry. It does not need to be long and I do hope it can serve for the American edition as now that England is doing them (they have been out of print for 8 years!) America will do them.

If you don't like the character of Telberg's photographs don't worry, just say so and I will find something else.

Hugo went off to Europe last night, and a few hours later I flew here to quiet, peace and atmosphere. But I can *work*.

I see you have moved. Send me a photo when you can.

When I come again—soon—we will make recordings of your readings and get you rich selling your records. Americans are lunatics about records.

Faber and Faber turned down *Children*. Owen is the publisher of Anna Kavan—do you know her? Miller, Cocteau, etc.

Always write to [the] Phoenix [bookshop in New York] for whatever books you want. Please read *Children* in the light of its brothers and sisters. I am trying *Mountolive* on a movie producer here.

A

In a letter from Peter Owen to Anaïs Nin dated November 18, 1958, he says: "Many thanks for telegraphing that Durrell is writing the preface for *Children of the Albatross*. We are ready to put the book in hand immediately and would certainly like to get it to the printer by the end of November. If you could let me know how long the preface is going to be, we could probably put it in hand a week or so before the preface arrives and arrange the preliminary pages accordingly, but if there is any deviation this might be awkward so if it is not going to be too long perhaps we could wait for the preface. If you could get it to us by the end of November, this would be wonderful. I don't suppose it is going to take ages to come through, or is it?" (Unpublished diary)

Los Angeles, November 21, 1958

Dear Larry:

Leaving New York with such precipitation as I had to help Hugo get off to Lausanne, I slipped Peter Owen's "hurry" letter to you so you would know he was rushing me. And just then got your card saying you would, so I cabled you. His wish was that your introduction might serve equally for America or England.

Today he writes me: "We are ready to put the book in hand immediately and would certainly like to get it to the printer by the end of December."

I wrote him to wait. I know how enormously busy you are. If you have loaned or lost the book (*Children of the Albatross*) you can get one from Marguerite Rebois.

I'm working hard at interesting people here—film people—in *Justine*—showing them *Mountolive*. The man Gore Vidal knew well and wrote films for, died. So Gore was ineffectual. But I am meeting others...and some I do know are not the right ones like that god of the commonplace Jerry Wald.[110]

Every day I make someone read *Justine* so my fan mail contains as many references to you as to myself.

As soon as I return to New York I will send you more selections for covers for your stories—if you don't like Telberg's photos.

Fanchette has saddened me by not writing to me.

There is a college where they read passages from *Justine*—that is what made me think of recording your own reading when we get together again.

The [Anaïs Nin] Press is slowly growing—do help me by directing whoever is looking for my books. It will form a basis to us publishing whatever we like later.

I enjoyed Claude's book—her humor—and I hear it's going well.

---

[110] American screenwriter and film producer.

I'm sorry I asked you to deviate even for a few minutes from your work...but no one else can do it.

R[upert] sends his love.

I don't suppose you'll be in Paris—Hugo wanted to see you. If you do go, call the Crillon—try if he is there. Office is in Lausanne 10 Avenue de la Gare, Lausanne.

My love to all. Is Claude all well again? How is the new house? Send me snapshots.

Love,

Anaïs

In a letter from Peter Owen to Anaïs Nin dated November 24, 1958, he says: "I see what you mean about not rushing Durrell, I know he is busy and it is nice of him to do the introduction. On the other hand, we can't do much about commencing production until we know when we are going to get the introduction. Have you any idea when it will be? If it is going to be within the next two or three weeks, that is fine, but if we would have to wait indefinitely, I wonder whether we should not proceed without it, possibly using it for the new book? Is he usually fairly prompt? You ask when are we going to publish *Children of the Albatross*. We want to publish it in March but of course we are tied to Durrell on this." (Unpublished diary)

Letter from Anaïs Nin to Hugh Guiler:
Los Angeles, December 8, 1958

Darling:

Yesterday enormously depressed by Durrell's introduction to English edition of *Children of the Albatross*...it seems out of proportion. Tell me what you think of it. I cut out the personal references. They were so flat and absurd. Why, why can't I get understanding of what I'm doing by either critics or other writers?

I took it hard. But I don't know why I *should* have expected Durrell to understand my work. I couldn't sleep. I'm afraid I'm still trying to make up for the fact that neither one of my parents ever said: "You're wonderful."

Only you have. And you, poor darling, have said it a million times.

Love,

A

Letter from Anaïs Nin to Hugh Guiler:
Los Angeles, December 10, 1958

Putting down all my expenses and paying with checks. So far the Anaïs Nin Press has a deficit!

After you read Durrell preface—if you feel as I do—I wish you'd call Peter Owen and ask him to not use it. I think its half-heartedness is worse than no preface, don't you?

I don't know why such lack of understanding still hurts me. *I have yours.*

Love,

A

[Los Angeles, December 1958]

Dear Larry:

It would have been so much better if you had written to me that you could not do the preface, did not like prefaces, were too busy, etc.!

I was not going to comment on it, but your letter today was rather irritable. Larry, first of all I would not have asked you for an introduction if I had not *needed* it, as I know you were busy. It was not because of your name or fame that I asked *you*, but because I had hoped, or imagined *you* understood my writing and would be the one to place proper focus on it. I explained to you that all these years in America I had received no evaluation at all, and that this had, in turn, affected Europe who wondered why I did not get any critical stature at all. But to the sadness of the disappointment in your total lack of understanding, came the added reproachfulness of your last letter—you are deluged in demands for blurbs, prefaces, etc. I was made to feel like one of your many nuisances. Also that bit about my ancient venerable reputation which you were teething in writing—I'm only 10 years older than you and I wrote *Winter of Artifice*, my first novel, after you wrote *The Black Book*, a most mature work.

I had the illusion that I occupied a special niche in your affection. For my friends I usually commit such foolish acts of devotion—both fictions were utterly demolished by your preface. Lines like "embalming" to distill essence, like being in a "casket" in grand hotels, soap bubbles applied to my work, conventional clichés about "feminine subjective" work, a certain disparagement and frivolity—were enough. But your letter today made matters worse. The basic shock was the non-caring and the distortion.

If you know that I had such a fantasy about your understanding or about your friendship, you should have refused to write.

I am not using the preface. It was a matter of great humiliation to me that my English publisher should think I needed to be introduced—but you greatly added to this.

I blame myself, however. I had imagined, invented and created something which did not exist.

My subjective feminine work is a long, careful work in which I am progressing from the dream outward as one way into relative truth.

Anaïs

Diary entry, Los Angeles, December 18, 1958: Christmas depression—disappointed in Durrell... (Unpublished diary)

In December 1958, Hugh Guiler, in a letter to Peter Owen, says: "Anaïs Nin says she is writing to Lawrence Durrell regarding preface which she requests you do not use." (Unpublished diary)

[New York, December 1958]

Dear Larry:

I'm so glad you wrote me as you did. I regretted my emotionalism which came out of a million accumulative distortions in twenty years of life in America, and which made me expect and count too deeply on your word. I realize so well you are overworked, had little time, and why should I have dreamt of the perfect preface? I don't want to go back to what hurt me. I value the alliance of the Three *Mousquetaires* too much. Let's just forget about it. Poor Peter Owen—he clung to the preface so desperately and I'm grateful you let me cut out what I felt to be detrimental (like the one about embalming to extract poetic essence?). I might add that your lightest word was the heaviest to digest—soap bubbles! I do not understand Peter's qualms anyway—*Spy* sold very well in England.

You don't mention anything about the film version of *Justine*. Has it come through? I'm seeing Gore today and will enquire.

Love to both of you,

Anaïs

Letter from Anaïs Nin to Hugh Guiler:
Los Angeles, December 26, 1958

Justine was sold to the movies, and this brought on a flood of tears, a real hour's weeping of the old childhood cry: "Why not me?" I'm glad for Durrell, who needs it badly financially. I'm glad and grateful we have our house and Bogner[111] to return to—for wholeness again.

Love,

A (Unpublished diary)

In a letter from Peter Owen dated January 7, 1959, he says: "As you know, I'm awfully keen on your work and want to do everything that will establish you here as one of the important contemporary writers. Therefore I do think in

---

[111] Dr. Inge Bogner was A.N.'s and H.G.'s psychoanalyst.

your interests that the Durrell introduction should be used. I think you tend to be biased against it because possibly he did not say quite what you wanted him to say, and partly because of the personal material he brought in which has now been cut out. Honestly, it reads very well now and I feel it is anything but half-hearted. Not to use it would be to discard what in effect is a valuable lever with the critics." (Unpublished diary)

Los Angeles, February 3, 1959

Dear Claude:

No, I didn't think when I sent the [stationery] that I would get such a charming letter! I would like to write longer letters but I haven't the energy.

My life would amuse you—when most women are content with *one*, I have two homes to take care of, two different lives, with many duties on both sides. In New York I help Hugo with his filmmaking, I run the Press, see friends, initiate people to New York life, take care of several young writers, read others' manuscripts; then I rush out here to Los Angeles and do housework, take care of Rupert's asthmatic father, follow [Rupert] to all his [string] quartets, sometimes help him correct papers or mark exams, take care of his dog, and try to write as well and copy and edit the diary. I write my letters while Rupert plays his viola—right now. Yesterday I saw Hugo off to Zürich, took an 8-hour flight to Los Angeles, arrived at dawn, surprised Rupert, went to the beach, cleaned the house, and tomorrow I'll be at my desk at 7 AM.

Will talk about the Preface someday, when I come again—I sent Jean [Fanchette] a booklet *On Writing*

[Alicat Bookshop, 1947] which contains my ideas so he may extract something from it for *Two Cities*. Larry and you are busy enough. But I see that I did not make it very clear that I cannot get published in America *at all* and that because of this, because I have received no critical or official evaluation of any kind; it has also prevented me from being published in Europe. Europe takes its "cue" from American sales, promotions, reviews, etc. It is a crucial situation. Doing my own publishing only takes care of the few people who want the books—1,000 or 2,000.

I know the day the Diary comes out this will change, but I did want to finish the novels.

I do wish when you go to Paris you ask the Ciné-matique to show you Hugo's films—so you will know Hugo the artist. Jean knows the people there, and I liked what he wrote about the films so much.

What I feel about my books, Claude, is that all everybody says [is] concern[ed] always with *externals*, how I write, etc., etc., whereas all that concerns me is that I have studied every *relationship*, that it is the complex relationships between human beings I have contributed to, pushing a little further into their meaning—as for example *Children of the Albatross* to me is [Raymond] Radiguet's *Devil in the Flesh* (millions of stories written about a woman and a boy) plus a deeper knowledge of what creates such relationships. This is what I had hoped Larry would put his finger on as he is concerned ultimately with same theme. All the rest—hues, style, poetry or not—is unessential to me, feminine or masculine. Also in our year of Lord Freud, we know everyone is subjective, and objectivity is a pretense.

When Lesley Blanch writes a marvelous book on 4 remarkable women (*Wilder Shores of Love*) and you get to know her, you realize *she* is in it too, of course.

You will have pleasure if Henry and Eve come in April. I love Eve without knowing her. I love you, Claude, for the same reason I love Eve—you are both intelligently loving wives, which is rare, the kind, as Varda[112] puts it, who help men create worlds.

I hope I can get over too—about same time. If you find me over-susceptible, please remember I have lived for 20 years in a hostile, barbaric country, cold-hearted, tough, brutal, chaotic and without insight and that I'm pretty damaged by it. It is a wonder I have kept my balance—and I'm longing to return to Europe ultimately. Forgive the susceptibility.

[Anaïs]

In a February 27, 1959 letter, after Nin approved the use of Durrell's preface, Peter Owen said: "The Durrell introduction to *Children*, I think, has served its purpose well. It is on the front flap of the jacket." (Unpublished diary)

Letter from Anaïs Nin to Hugh Guiler:
Los Angeles, March 26, 1959

Reviews of *Mountolive* say it is boring—that Durrell has gone into *political clichés* as motivation for action. This criticism from America is too funny when for twenty

---

[112] Jean Varda (1893-1971) was a painter and collagist befriended by A.N. and H.M.

years they have written only in terms of political clichés, and *Time* magazine complains of a lack of inner motivation!! Well, it aroused, at least, my humor. I had a good belly laugh. And I, always damned for my inner research!

[Anaïs] (Unpublished diary)

[New York, March 1959]
Mount Sinai Hospital

Dear Claude and Larry:

Here I am recovering from double pneumonia (Spanish extravagance) and catching up with my correspondence.

This month I gave all my energy to *Two Cities* which will be good for all of us. And what do you think of another February in our family (Jean's little girl)?

I meant to write you—perhaps I already did—to thank you particularly for introducing me to Jean Fanchette. His friendship is a delight.

Claude—where did your book appear? In America or England? Did you mean the one I read, or a new one?

Larry—curious that you spoke of sprouting, and of many healings due to Claude and France. My summation of you, Larry, when I left in the train was: he is a wounded man. But I didn't know how deeply.

Irony is I didn't know [the] extent of damage done by life in America. Jean seems to be healing that fast—almost completely.

Until I get the magazine I won't be able to get as many subscriptions as we need. I'm better at giving than taking so I'm surrounded by misers who look startled when I say please subscribe! And American writers won't write for no pay so I'm having trouble getting writers. They are all so spoiled and commercial.

Hugo came back with most incredible [movie] shots of Venice—a poem. He can find the unknown face of every city.

I'm not sure I'll be able to go over until May—because of precarious health.

It will be good for Henry to go over, certainly for Eve.

What do you hear from Hollywood? I'll be there March 20. What shall I say to people who ask me about *The Black Book*?

In your preface, the Grand Hotel childhood amused me. What a fantasy! We were poor, a musician's family. My father at 20 was professor of Schola Cantorum, Paris. When he left us and my mother's small income [was] gone, we were poorer, and in America that means unromantically so. When I married Hugo we were poor too—I supported Henry for 10 years by [self-] denials, not out of luxury. Only the last five or six years have we been comfortable. Even if I could have, I would not be raised in a jewel casket!

I think you confused my life with [the description of] my father in *Winter of Artifice*. I realized your fantasy when you spoke of the Diaries delivered by a *chauffeur*. We did not even have a car in France! But if you like this story's version better than the truth—*c'est votre droit! Ça c'est le grand romancier!* [that's your right! You are the great novelist!]

Wearing a red Arabian burnouse in the hospital to cheer them up. And people bring paintings and tapestries instead of flowers so it looks like an art gallery. [During] the last "session" the king of the gypsies was ill too, and

600 camped outside as per tradition, and made my stay delightful—disrupting all discipline. The interest here is that it is half-negro, half-white—unusual in America—and that gives it a South Sea island atmosphere—the negroes never accepted the impersonality of Americans. They spend their off time in my room. I never have to ring. All emergency calls are made in my room, where they are sure to be found. 10 days of jail!

À *bientôt*, love,

Anaïs

[En route to Los Angeles, March 1959]

Dear Larry:

Such a wonderful letter from you. Just as I was going to write you how elated I was at *Mountolive* being selected [for the] Book of the Month Club. And Henry's *Tropics* permitted to be sold. America is becoming civilized.[113]

I write you on the plane, flying to Los Angeles. So weak I can't carry a handbag—but intensity of New York was preventing me from convalescing—and R[upert] was getting desperate. My only outing was a visit to Varda because he wanted me so much to see his paintings before he takes them back to Sausalito, California. *He* cannot live in New York. He is a marvelous painter—he never left the fairytale—white-haired and so

---

[113] Although efforts were underway to legally publish H.M.'s Paris novels, which were banned in America, it would be another two years before the courts granted permission.

battered by life. His Greek wife is giving him up, and they gave a party to celebrate divorce!

I am working hard at distributing *Two Cities*, collecting subscriptions, etc. Sent 1,400 announcements to University libraries.

Los Angeles: Rupert sends his love.

The pneumonia has made my trip [to France] impossible—by the time I can travel Hugo will be back.

Don't feel badly about the preface anymore. I know exactly how it happened. Owen rushed you. You were in the middle of a book, with personal harassments, moving, children, correspondence, and in no mood for it. You opened a bottle of wine and out of friendship set out to do something you were in no mood to do. No time to reread books, etc. Also you didn't know how important it was, crucial, etc. It was for America. England can read. But America has no inner evaluations, only what other people say.

I will write to Eve about Nîmes, etc., but I don't think you need to be concerned about Henry. It is Eve, I feel, who wants to live, not to be isolated and a cook-hostess to whoever wants to come. But she will have her time in Paris.

Love to you and Claude,
Anaïs

[Los Angeles, May 1959]

Dear Claude and Larry:

How I wish I could have joined you this spring—to celebrate reunions, to talk over *Two Cities*, to celebrate the success of *Mountolive*.[114] I want to write in *T.C.* about the early meetings, [from] pages out of the Diary, but was critical of [the] writing, not good enough I thought. You must be enjoying Henry and Eve's visit.

I feel badly that Peter did not send you the cut preface—it should have been submitted to you for approval! He was in such a hurry—why, I don't know—I hope you were not bothered, dear Larry.

Rupert and I just returned from sitting on the site he chose to build a home, following true California tradition—overlooking a small lake, with mountains in the back. He is fulfilling a long, old fantasy. He will build this summer.

I'll be in New York May 11. Write me there at 35 West 9th New York City 11. Soon you will have all the children again and no time for letters.

Working on 1,000 pages these 6 weeks—but had to give up the Press—no strength.

How is your book doing, Claude?[115] I never read reviews or magazines or newspapers so I never know—and have been away from New York. I wanted to ask Varda to do a cover for "Snow"—he is so wonderful. Henry will tell you—but he will leave soon after I return.

Do you remember the little village where we waited for you before visiting the gypsy sea place of the miracles? We bought black espadrilles and every time we wear them to the beach we talk about our visit.

---

[114] L.D. had gone to Paris in early May to promote the French edition of *Balthazar*.

[115] A possible reference to *A Chair for the Prophet* (Faber, 1959).

I hope you'll have a happy summer. Please try and see Hugo's films at Cinématique if you go to Paris.

My love,

Anaïs

In a letter from Lawrence Durrell to Anaïs Nin written in May 1959, he says: "I'm glad the English edition opened things up [for you]; I knew you had a small but choice public in U.K. and that Owen was right to believe he could expand it steadily. You'll see, it will roll up." (Unpublished diary)

[Los Angeles, early summer 1959]

Dear Claude and Larry:

I hope you're having a marvelous summer. I'll be in Europe in July but not in France. Going to Italy to help Hugo finish his new film in Venice.

But for the moment I'm in Los Angeles, working quietly. New York was so intense and full. Saw Varda. Henry will tell you about him—attended his "divorce" party from Chrissa. He remains as lyrical and poetic as ever, sailing transparently, in all his oriental colors, through all catastrophes.

A Frenchman translated a bit of the *The Subterraneans* by Kerouac which I sent you as a curiosity, a *collier d'os barbare* [barbaric bone necklace], but which Henry praised wildly.

I can understand your discussion about Olympia [Press] and *The Black Book*. But will Olympia refuse to sell in America? America's commercials have their eyes fixed on Girodias.

We're all praying for the film!

Rupert is very happy, building his home, and I secretly trying to find him a marvelous girl. Our cycle is ending. It was a happy one—but Hugo always wins by depth and endurance—a deeper current. Something people like Fred will never understand—there are eternal loves and transient ones—there are some time cannot corrode, and some which are illusory. I played a role to make R[upert] happy for 10 years. A marvelous illusion.

À plus tard—love from the 3 of us,

Anaïs

[P.S.] Sending you a letter for Henry...[116]

[Paris, July 29, 1959]

[Larry:]

Sad to be in Paris without you and Henry and Eve. Worked hard on film in Venice, returning to Los Angeles—hope to be back in September.

Jean Fanchette and I talk by the hour about you—so I know all is wonderful, marvelous, *extrordinaire*. I wish I could stay here. Did you ever see the Well house—a real *puit* [well] with a Black Angel covering at the bottom!

Love to all,

Anaïs

---

[116] Henry and Eve Miller and Alfred and Anne Perlès were visiting the Durrells in June 1959.

[New York, September 1959]

Dear Claude and Larry:

Not a word from Nîmes all summer! So it must have been either such a marvelous one that you forgot everyone else, or such a strenuous one, or a delirious one, or whatever it was. I am sorry to have missed it. As Larry said everything depends on one's interpretation of silence! Waiting for *Clea*.

So out of touch while traveling and out west. And I never read reviews or magazines so I do not know. I'm so glad to have [your new] preface to *The Black Book*—a nibble for those who can't get the book.[117] I would love to have news. I came back with *Black Books* hidden among the dresses and was not censored.

Hugo made his film in Venice, sounds and all.

And here we are—visitors from India and Sweden, a reading and presentation of films at an off-Broadway theatre—listening to praise of you, watching Swedish films, burdened with work for *Two Cities*, active, multilateral. Hugo did not make his *grand coup de fortune*, so no more [private] publishing.

I hope when the children are in school you will find time for a transatlantic *pneumatique*.

I wrote to Henry, to Eve…

We think of you, love,

Anaïs

---

[117] L.D. wrote a new preface for the 1959 Olympia Press edition, which was also used in the Dutton edition the following year.

Letter from Anaïs Nin to Wallace Fowlie:
Los Angeles, April 1960

Dear Wallace:

I was disappointed in *Clea*, for all the reasons you give. I feared this already when I read *Balthazar*. The day we began our deepest talk I was intending to ask you: do you think he will ever go deeper? He remained the poet amorous of externals, knowing passion for woman and city but not love, not insight. Illusion is passion but love is clairvoyant and truly knows the other. You state it absolutely accurately when you say: "Don't you think that love has the power of greatest transformation so that love which exists between two people is something greater than simply the sum of the individuals, a mathematical absurdity, a metaphysical certainty?"

Yes I do, and more, behind the illusion created by our needs, myth-making true love discovers a human being and loves more. I feel Durrell created a shallow world of fraudulent relationships. *Justine* was the chant of an enamored poet and thus beautiful. And this is true according to my knowledge of him as a human being.

I may fail as Durrell did in a deeper sense. I may fail too but I am trying to go deeper and deeper. We have had so much of surface.

Anaïs (Unpublished diary)

[Paris, June 1960]

Dear Larry:

So pleased to hear from you and amused by the letters you enclosed. Hope you pensioned off *Justine*![118] Larry, we missed each other. Yes, I know what it is to be under a mountain of correspondence. Just returned from Stockholm where I went to return love and devotion they have given me, and they gave me such a royal welcome that I almost collapsed from exhaustion. Met fascinating people, was introduced by [editor Artur] Lundkvist and called pinup girl of literature.

What more? Hugo's films were wonderfully understood and commented [on]. We spent time with Ingrid Theullin and her husband—met the nephew of Isak Dinesen—but had no energy to go on to Copenhagen. Now same thing at Brussels—until middle of June when we go to Venice to finish film.

Our love to both of you,
Anaïs

Letter (fragment) from Anaïs Nin to Hugo Raes:[119]
Los Angeles, November 1960

Dear Hugo:

They say Henry Miller will settle in Europe so you may meet. I think he wants a change of cycle, following his divorce from the best wife he ever had, and an escape

---

[118] *Justine* would be made into a film released in 1969.

[119] A Belgian writer and friend of A.N.

from the lack of respect America gives him, official, I mean. It hurts him to see Durrell get so much official recognition.

[Anaïs] (Unpublished diary)

Letter (fragment) from Anaïs Nin to Roger Bloom: [120]
[Los Angeles, December 1960]

[Roger:]

I think Henry went to Paris to make a break from the loss of Eve. He felt that, I hear. And at his age I doubt if he will marry again. [121] I think he also felt badly about the easy way in which Durrell got acclaim, and what it took Miller thirty years to get, and even then, the real open, official respect comes to him in Europe. America has never said things about him openly, nor is, I believe, proud of him. I know one critic who thinks well of him but does not dare [say so]. But I am sure he will come back for the sake of his children, as he can only see them in the summer and I doubt if he will be able to pay their way to Europe every summer.

Grove Press wanted to publish the *Cancer*, but it is Henry who refused. I think he recoiled from the kind of three-ring circus which was accorded *Lady Chatterley* in New York at the time of the trial. In England it was more or less dignified, but in N.Y. it was a show that was most humiliating to writers and critics.

[Anaïs] (Unpublished diary)

---

[120] An unfairly convicted felon championed by H.M. and A.N.

[121] Indeed, H.M. married his fifth wife, Hoki Tokuda, in 1967.

Letter (fragment) from Anaïs Nin to Roger Bloom:
[1961]

[Roger:]

About Durrell I haven't written you frankly, because I would not want Henry to know and then Durrell should know. I loved *Justine* but none of the other books. I don't share the popular idea that he is the greatest writer of our time. I'm afraid inflation of writers is part of our commercialism and part of the fact that 90% of the people follow the bestsellers—and they read what they are told to read. He is overrated. But please keep this to yourself. I see that you cannot be taken in by a writer's aura of public adoption! That is good. You judge for yourself.

[Anaïs] (Unpublished diary)

Letter from Anaïs Nin to Marguerite Young:[122]
Los Angeles, February 6, 1963

Dear Marguerite:

My renewed friendship with Miller was a Proustian experience. It was as if when I loved him I saw only one side of him, and now in friendship, the other side. The negative. I have yet to see him as the world sees him. In both him and Durrell I see this frightening lack of empathy, lack of insight into others. They live in a world completely fabricated. Perhaps analysis has made me feel that such fabrications add to the blindness of the world,

---

[122] Friend of A.N. and author of *Miss MacIntosh, My Darling* (1965).

and I expect something clairvoyant from writers. And then I wonder, perhaps that is not what people seek from a writer, clairvoyance, only fiction to add to the fictions they live with and by. Never have I observed before the fiction which love creates, the illusion, for example, of his honesty and simplicity as when I see Miller today unhappy and alone with the world loving him, but he is somehow unable to accept it. Feeling guilt, as he says.

[Anaïs] (Unpublished diary)

[Paris, April 1964]

Dear Larry and Claude:

When I arrived I found *Spy* all printed and a quotation André Bay[123] found in my diary which he has been reading. I was shocked that he had not asked your permission to quote you, as I know neither of you nor Henry care much about my books. The extraordinary liberties they take:

He changed the gender of the title without consulting me, etc.[124] I hope you will forgive me. He is reading diaries.

I'll be here two weeks as Marguerite Duras will work on a script if she likes the director.[125] *If* by any chance you'll be in Paris it would be *marvelous* to see you both!

---

[123] An editor at a prospective French publisher, Éditions Stock.

[124] *Une espionne dans la maison de l'amour* [*A Spy in the House of Love*] was changed from *Un espion...*

[The passage in] question reads (written long ago): *"Quel écrivain vous êtes! J'ai toujours rêvé d'un idéal en littérature que seule une femme pouvait attendre..."* [What a writer you are! I always dreamed of an ideal in literature that only a woman could expect...] Out of context (you were writing about the "Birth" story), it sounds different! *Quel monde!*

I saw Henry in Los Angeles. He looked well—wanted Elizabeth Taylor to act in his play.[126]

[Anaïs]

New York, April 18, 1966

Dear Claude and Larry:

Harcourt Brace sent you a copy of the *Diary*, and so did I, so give the extra one to Frédéric-Jacques Temple—there's a lot about Henry in it.[127] Larry makes a charming appearance in the volume to follow and I will send extracts concerning you for your approval. You can be in or out as you please. I hope *this* volume, which you read in its original complete state, will please you as your comments in 1930s were generous and prescient. I hope this will renew our friendship.

---

[125] A.N. fought vainly for years to have *A Spy in the House of Love* made into a movie.

[126] Following the premiere of H.M.'s *Just Wild about Harry* in Italy in July 1963, the subsequent production in Edinburgh, Scotland, was closed down on the second night on grounds of obscenity.

[127] The first volume of *The Diary of Anaïs Nin*.

I saw you on television—on your island. I saw Henry in Los Angeles at an exhibit of his water colors. I hear you made a film! Is it true Jean Garrique is writing your biography? She gave me the most beautiful review in *The New York Times*—thank god. Sending you a photo of the Diaries as in the book they cropped the mountainous pile.

Love,

Anaïs

New York, November 3, 1966

Dear Larry:

Sorry I can't supply boudoir scenes just now! Please answer me: I want to spare you reading [the second volume of the] diary, sections portraying our meetings in Paris—would you like to trust me as Henry did on the second volume after seeing how much people like him after it? I quote a few letters on writing matters, all of it very loving and not one derogatory word—all charm and understanding, etc. Or would you like to see every word before you give permission? Let me know, won't you, while I'm in New York so I can cut out just what concerns you and send it as after that I go on lectures, etc.

How did you proceed with the H.M. correspondence?[128] How do you feel about being written about? I have a lovely photo of you of that period.

Love,

Anaïs

---

[128] This is most likely a reference to *Lawrence Durrell and Henry Miller: A Private Correspondence* (Dutton, 1963), edited by George Wickes.

Los Angeles, December 5, 1966

Dear Larry:

Stopped in the middle of copying such a beautiful letter from you written during the war from Greece, because I was once more pained by the great change in you towards me and would like to understand it before it is recorded in later diaries as a mystery. (Such a beautiful letter. I would like to quote it in *Diary* volume 3—working on it now—but I imagine you may want to edit some of it.)

The great contrast between your opinions, reactions, understanding and deep friendship, and later attitudes. In the diary of 1934-1939 as I told you, all is trust and understanding. What happened?

When I became for a few years estranged from Henry, when he moved to Big Sur, everything connected with him was painful, and I felt he was essentially *your* friend and you *his*, and I ceased writing to you. Did I offend you then? I cannot believe the mere dislike of my novels could create such a chasm. Did you feel I had deserted you? In Paris when I invited you to come and see me, did I offend you by saying it could not be the Crillon because the Crillon bill was paid by the Company, not by me, and was not within my means? By the time I came to visit you [in 1958] there was a wall of some kind. Vague remarks.

You thought I had been unkind to Henry (from the *Diary* you can see I was not). I tried not to see the misunderstandings but they appeared clear when you wrote the parody of a preface which so wounded me. And even then I thought perhaps you had disliked my books so much. But now the diary, the same diary you loved so much *before*, and you find nothing to love, nothing to respond to, you find only flaws. In cuts which were humanly necessary...you are concerned about Fred, but were you concerned when Fred wrote such an absurd story of my relationship to Henry? Did you worry then about whether he was just? I think I was very kind to him. He caused me great humiliation and almost destroyed all my protection of H[ugo].

You recently wrote to me about my vulnerability. You thought I had left it out as well as humor, playfulness, but in Paris you spoke of the tragic quality of the diary and did not expect comedy. If you know about the vulnerability, how could you then do everything which could possibly wound it? *Mystère.*

The second visit I paid you I felt something wrong. Tell me what happened. I know (I found out by accident) *The New York Times* asked you to write about the *Diary* and you refused. Henry did too. But Henry felt he was too close to it, too involved. Friends who visit you tell me of your reserved comments on me. Others like Mai Zetterling[129] bring me your love. Musketeers, Henry, yourself and me, later it is Fred who claims to be the third.

Please be truthful, dear Larry, for the sake of the old sincerity. I do not wish to record sad changes, betrayals, some misunderstanding. Is it my fault? Have I been remiss?

---

[129] Swedish actress-turned-director and friend of L.D., who would marry David Hughes, author of *Himself and Other Animals* (about Gerald Durrell, L.D.'s brother).

I had hoped we would have a talk, but it looks as if I would not come to Europe again. I have found greater affinities with Japan, a deeper relationship to its writers, critics.

I thought you understood the human motivations for what I could not tell. Close friends were happy that I could publish *any* part at all, knowing otherwise the diary would have been buried for fifty years.

Won't you take the time and patience to clarify and restore a friendship which was so precious to me?

[Anaïs]

In a letter from Lawrence Durrell to Anaïs Nin dated September 3, 1967, he says, upon reading Diary 2, *in which he is portrayed prominently:* "I was terribly touched by the little dedication to me and hope sometime soon to redeem the epithet charming which in same mysterious way seems to have foundered—though what went wrong, when and how, I have no clue. Sometimes one quite inadvertently hurts friends and loses them without meaning to, without wanting to, and spends the rest of their life in puzzled me-fulness, chewing the cud and wondering. Not me. *Toujours*, here I am, your old friend." (Unpublished diary)

[New York] September 17, 1970

Dear Larry:

May I ask you a favor which is very easy to respond to. Hugh has chosen to be out of the *Diary*. He also prefers to be known as the filmmaker Ian Hugo. He was never rich, or a *mécène* [patron]; he worked in a bank;

Louveciennes was rented, not owned; we supported several relatives. He is distressed by your repeated references to him in a most trivial way which is not necessary to your recollections—of his wines or his non-existent fortune. It is not really much of a detail which it would please him (and of course also Anaïs who has had to refute this legend for years). I know those considerations don't weigh much in your friendships. If you must really mention this short stay could then spell his name HUGH GUILER or as an artist then IAN HUGO.

Your reference once more in Dylan Thomas preface offends Hugh and Ian and me as it is pure fiction.[130]

Please.

Anaïs

[New York] October 9, 1970

Dear Larry:

I'm so glad you wrote me a charming letter. I was going to add some of the side effects of this "legend of wealth." The journalists started to include you among the protégées, which I vigorously objected to. I told in the *Diary* how you paid for publication of *Winter of Artifice*. It was this money I tried to return to you at our first meeting in France and which you misunderstood. Anyone who reads [the] *Diary* carefully could see if I had

---

[130] An excerpt from L.D.'s essay "Shades of Dylan Thomas" (1957) reads: "Anaïs Nin's husband, Hugo Guiler the painter, also happened to be Hugo Guiler the banker and patron of the arts; he allowed us to make his London flat our headquarters and thoughtfully furnished it with six cases of a good Bordeaux."

been rich I would not have given up Louveciennes which I loved for a 2-room apartment, nor the car, nor the Spanish maid. If I had been rich I would not have borrowed from Fraenkel to print *House of Incest*. The truth is Hugo lost all in the stock market and indebted us for life. Anyone who really reads the *Diary* could understand, but it suited Henry's fictionalized life and soothed his guilt.[131] It was a destructive legend. I who hated wealth and the bourgeois world. It was sad to sit at the Cinématique and [its] recognition of Hugo as a filmmaker and have someone bring up the Thomas anthology. It was like Henry who can only say on the telephone that I was his guardian angel, not a writer, a woman, a person. Just a protector! Damn it, Larry, you are sensitive enough to understand how twisted that is.

I began to disbelieve in your friendship for many reasons—one [was] a nasty letter you wrote to me which I didn't answer because of [Claude's death of cancer].

I would like to believe in it again. On the basis of your last letter I will try.

Anaïs

[Los Angeles] November 19, 1973

Dear Larry:

So that we can enjoy each other's company let me catch you up on some necessary data. In 1947 Hugo and I separated amicably. In 1947 he resigned from the bank.

---

[131] A.N. believed that H.M. assuaged his guilt over taking money from the Guilers for more than a decade by convincing himself that they were rich.

Which means I am no longer a banker's wife. I have been living with Rupert Pole, since then.[132] Hugo also made the decision to be left out of the *Diary*. So those who are his friends make as little reference to the relationship as possible, which also enables me to continue my support of him as a filmmaker. Because I had to leave him out of the *Diary* at his specific wish, people tend to ask questions. I would be grateful if you sympathized with Hugo's wishes and did not answer that whenever possible.

I will certainly see you at Henry's, but as in the past you flatly contradicted my statements (that I was never wealthy, that someone who works for a bank at a salary is not a banker and that I never owned a Henry Moore [painting] but that Hugo's sister worked with him in London and that may have been where the wish to own one might have come from Hugo). I feel uneasy about giving you my home address and inviting you until I am sure you will not cause me embarrassment [as] in the past. (Preface to Dylan Thomas.) You fictionalized my life (child of palace hotels) and that is what made our friendship so difficult the past years. Please apply a little human consideration instead of your beautiful imagination to my life at the present.

Love,

Anaïs

---

132 While A.N. and H.G. were apart in much of 1947, there was no mutually-agreed-upon separation; H.G. did resign from the bank but became active in banking again shortly thereafter. A.N. and R.P. spent roughly half of each year together until the 1960s when A.N. began to favor Los Angeles as her home.

[Los Angeles] November 29, 1973

Dear Larry:

I have the most enchanting description of my first visit to Sommières, absolutely glowing with gayety and richness. I will show it to you when you come. I hear you have married, and I am happy as I think you were lonely. Also the only way to shut out the invasion from the world is to have a strong personal world to hide in. I have much to tell you as the diary I am working on now, 1958, is full of the best chapter of our friendship.

To finish the tiresome subject of wealth. H. never earned more than $10,000 or at the most $12,000 a year. What gave the illusion of wealth was that we traveled at the expense of his firm, who paid hotels and trips, and places like the Crillon. It was all a façade. The other is a more subtle one, that H. was haunted by the American dream of wealth and loved to put on a bluff, loved to inflate his work. He never achieved it. But he had the "air." Mostly on an expense account. The usual American façade. Now that is all over.

Let us finish with that. It was a painful subject for me because that was not what I wanted, or really was, and only the artist life meant anything to me. I thought you knew that.

But let's remember only the good moments. I also have a beautiful letter from you concerning your own work, and comments on mine. I will show you. When are you coming?

Love,
Anaïs

Diary excerpt, Los Angeles, December 1, 1973: In 1958 I decided that Durrell is a brilliant cheat who does not have a deep knowledge of character. It shows in *Balthazar*, a *soi-disant* psychiatrist. He promised relativity of truth, but that lies in acceptance of subjectivity and that means introspection, going inward, and he has not.

The deep disappointment at finding out Durrell does not understand me or my work.

Why should he, I say in 1973. He is superficial and lives in fiction. Like Henry, he invents. He does not see. Typical of his lack of art for relationship is the legend of my wealth which he clings to, and all I can obtain from him is a courteous promise not to embarrass me when he comes to Los Angeles, but never *hearing* what I tell him. (Unpublished diary)

On December 12, 1973, Durrell wrote to Nin: "My Dear Anaïs. [...] Have just finished a queer novel[133] and am in the usual state of exhilarated depression—the state we all know only too well. It seems curious to be married again after nearly seven years of bachelorhood. But at sixty-two one can't make plans I feel. Just take things as they come.

"I gather [...] that you have accepted the limited tutorial scheme fostered by the Whitney Institute. It's marvelous, I think, and am hoping it will work for me; to earn one's living by staying right at home seems too good

---

[133] *Monsieur*, the first of the five novels in *The Avignon Quintet*.

to be true. We shall see if I can make the grade."[134] (Unpublished diary)

Tahiti, December 22, 1973

Dear Larry:

Travel & Leisure the magazine you wrote for once sent me to Tahiti for 10 days. I don't know when you are planning to come to Los Angeles. I hope I won't miss seeing you before you go to Pasadena. I return Jan. 2 or 3. Will phone at Henry's.

This was a godsend. I was overworking and now I'm in paradise.

Love,
Anaïs

[Los Angeles, May 1974]

Dear Larry:

Do you still feel like annihilating Binion on Lou? This would be a good time as Peters' biography is being reprinted in paperback.[135]

Wanted to tell you I'm well again.

---

[134] In mid-December 1973 L.D. and his fourth wife Ghislaine (de Boysson) came to Los Angeles, and from January to March 1974 lectured at CalTech in Pasadena. On February 27 he spent his 62nd birthday with A.N. and H.M.; on March 16 A.N. attended his final seminar, shortly after which the Durrells left. A.N. and L.D. would not see each other again.

[135] L.D. detested Rudolf Binion's biography on Lou Andreas-Salomé; A.N. wrote the preface to the paperback reprint of H.F. Peters' version.

Did Stock send Ghislaine the other diaries?
All our love,
Anaïs

Los Angeles, June 3, 1974

Dear Larry:

I can only plead overwork for misaddressing my letter to you. Richard Centing wants to devote a whole issue to you in the Newsletter (enclosed).[136] I felt your essay on Binion versus Peters would be too important to place in the Newsletter (which goes to 500 libraries) so I talked to *The New York Times* about your interest in the Peters biography which will come out in paperback with a preface by me, but they expressed reluctance at reviewing a reprint. They hardly glance at paperbacks, so if I don't find a more worthy place, the Newsletter will be proud to do it. (I will try [Robert] Kirsch of the *Los Angeles Times* and let you know.) We must synchronize the Newsletter with your novel. Do you know the publication date?

My love to both of you, the deepest,
Anaïs

Diary excerpt, Paris, November 8, 1974: Durrell's new book [*Monsieur*] distressing: top heavy with ideas; impossible human beings; intellectual games; superb descriptive writing; depiction of neurosis without the slightest insight; words empty; Edgar Allan Poe situa-

---

[136] The "newsletter" was the quarterly *Under the Sign of Pisces: Anaïs Nin and her Circle* (Ohio State University Libraries).

tions; lack of unity; obsession with death unresolved; handled with sensational exoticism; he can only describe Alexandria; no feeling for the meta-physical...

Summation: *Trompe d'oeil.*

I was bored. Fell asleep reading it. (Unpublished diary)

Diary excerpt, Paris, November 11, 1974: Telephone from Durrell and Ghislaine. Larry asks: "How do you maintain your energy? At 60 I feel like fainting away." [...] I can't tell him: don't drink.[137] [...]

Those I hope will never write about me because they do not know me at all: Miller; Vidal; Durrell. (Unpublished diary)

Los Angeles, September 10, 1975

Dear Larry:

Your letter to Swallow [Press] pleased me deeply. If you could write all this about two lectures you must have *wanted* to praise me. I was very touched.

It all came like a bouquet of flowers after *nine* months of fighting cancer. I am recovering but energy is very low. I managed to finish Vol. 6 with help—remembered your generous cable: "Carte Blanche" when I asked if you wanted to see what I wrote about you. *Pas contre* Lesley Blanch, whose portrait was done with love, refused to allow any of it except my praise of her work!

---

[137] L.D. had taken to drinking great amounts of wine, sometimes leading to drunken tirades and physical abuse of his wife.

Your visit (with Ghislaine) last year was such a joy. I wish we had more time to talk. It was too frustrating not seeing you in Paris and our parties one block away from each other.[138]

The writing in *Monsieur* was as magical as ever. You appear again in Vol. 6.

Love,

Anaïs

[Los Angeles, April 1976]

Dear Larry:

As you probably know my brother Joaquín did all his musical studies in Paris so when he came to visit me we discussed your letter. I thought I would send you his letter; it might be useful. His reference to "vague improvesations" is to two young men whose music I have: a clarinetist and pianist who have been concertizing in Japan, France, etc.[139]

Do write me more about your projects. I talked with Henry who was really hurt by Brassaï's stupid book.[140]

---

[138] On November 4, 1974, A.N. writes in her diary: "Durrell was having an opening the same day, same hour! Ghislaine came to embrace me for a moment" (unpublished diary).

[139] Ghislaine tried to organize a TV production of A.N.'s *House of Incest* with a script by L.D. In his April 28, 1976 letter to A.N., Joaquín Nin-Culmell suggests using a "professional composer" for the musical soundtrack, not "just some musical improvisations by a relatively inexperienced performer, however gifted" (unpublished diary).

[140] *Henry Miller: grandeur nature* (Gallimard, 1975).

But he is well and pleased with reactions to his book of friends.

Love to you both,

Anaïs

Los Angeles, April 12, 1976 (telegram)

Nothing could please me more than to have you do my first TV treatment. You have 6 months option for *House of Incest* and my blessing forever.

Love,

Anaïs

[Los Angeles, May 1976]

Dear Larry:

Rereading your first card I realized I had made it clear I do give you an *option ami* for as long as you please.

House of Incest pleases me but is more difficult. Stories from *Under a Glass Bell* may be easier.

In any case, I'm very proud that it is you doing it and trust you completely.

Love to you and Ghislaine,

[Anaïs]

Los Angeles, May 18, 1976

Dear Larry and Ghislaine:

The clarinet player is sending you a tape for you to hear and judge. I rejoice at all your activities.

A specialist-selected television *équipe*, with Maurice the painter and Dumayet the interviewer, are coming in July to do a series of interviews for each diary. I wish Ghislaine could join them.

Henry and I talk over the telephone as I can't leave the house. Too much radiation damaged me and caused a fistula which prevents me from going anywhere. Otherwise I feel well enough to work on the last diary, [volume] 7.

I am sending you volume 6 which has photographs of you and family and story of my visit to you.

The diaries and letters have been bought by UCLA. Some will be sealed, the early ones open. It will help with all the medical expenses.

Typing four or five pages a day and interesting visitors make the days short. And of course in this house one does not mind being shut in.

It sounds as if you were entering a new cycle.

The translation of *Under a Glass Bell* is even better.

Everyone asks about you and hopes you will come again. My love to you both,

Anaïs

Los Angeles, May 20, 1976

Dear Larry:

Your beautiful letter about the possibilities of *H of I* appealed to me very much: to *create* an atmosphere, abstract. You are right in suggesting Fez, Mexico, etc. How I wish we could discuss it all—but perhaps it is best that your own rich imagination be given utter freedom.

About music, I sent you my brother's advice and a highly gifted clarinetist whose music evokes the Inca flute.

I am so sad that my illness imprisons me. Too much radiation for the cancer opened a fistula which has to be cared for all the time. It is like a perpetual abscess—incurable. Fortunately I can work, take walks and receive visitors who bring music, films to the house.

All my M.S. are going to UCLA with your and Henry's papers. June 2 we deliberate the contract.

Will Ghislaine act in *H of I*?

Diary 6 is late but you will get it soon.

My love to both of you,

Anaïs

Los Angeles, August 15, 1976

Dear Ghislaine:

Your letter delighted me. I admire Mai Zetterling tremendously. I saw her two films at a private showing. I caught a glimpse of her in N.Y. She is strong and a superb director. I'm so happy at all the news you give me that I am sure it accelerated my cure. The treatment is a Japanese vaccine and I am responding to it. A French cancer specialist over the telephone said it was the best treatment he knew.

Recovery is slow. But I can do a little work on Vol. 7—and I swim and walk. Only I can't leave the house so you'll have to come and visit me. You know how both Rupert and I fell in love with you! I would like a photograph of you for diary 7. Mai had planned a visit.

Je vous embrasse bien fort,

Anaïs

Anaïs Nin, 1969.

EPILOGUE

When Anaïs Nin visited Paris in late 1974 as part of a book promotion tour, she was already aware that she had potentially serious health problems. Not only was it her final trip overseas, it was also the last time she would see her legal husband, Hugh Guiler.[141] By the end of the year, she was diagnosed with advanced cancer, the complications of which nearly incapacitated her and seriously interfered with her editing of the diaries. She felt the cruelty of a physically ravaging disease marring her life at a time when she could have been relishing her success and working on new projects.

During her illness, Nin remained in Los Angeles with Rupert Pole, who went to great lengths to care for her and make her comfortable. Despite the efforts of doctors, drugs, alternative healers, friends and legions of well-wishers, Anaïs Nin died on January 14, 1977.

Letter from Lawrence Durrell to Rupert Pole:
Sommières, February 7, 1977[142]

It seems appropriate, Rupert, that I should address a message to the shade of Anaïs care of you, since so often during the last years she told us (and when we were with

---

[141] A.N. and H.G. stayed in separate hotels; hers was covered by her publisher and his by his employer.

[142] The text was meant to be read as a eulogy at A.N.'s memorial service.

you, we saw) how greatly your devoted magnanimity helped her surmount the ravages of her illness in order to continue her work on the diaries upon which her future renown will depend. I myself knowing her pretty well, and knowing how fragile her patrician spirit was—so easily hurt, so easily cast down by a rebuff by someone insensitive—could not help but marvel at the frightening tenacity and singleness of purpose which drove her on, kept her on course. In all this it was the stout right arm and the chivalrous self-abnegation of yourself, Rupert, which made possible this massive attack on the central citadels of art by this beautiful witch-like woman whom we called our third Musketeer. So we have lost our woman Musketeer, and the loss is psychically a heavy one for this small group of friends! She was our Aramis—the slim and delicate and aristocratic one, the born duelist. We lumbered about around her busy about our own work. But Anaïs was always there with some vital message, something which awoke and informed us, something which enriched us—she was quite inexhaustible when it came to giving; in a curious sort of way she managed to enrich herself by this constant dedication to her friends, and when there was no way in which she could be of use to someone she fell into a despondency.

She had the grand style in her life and in her work. She told me how she had at last learned the bitter lesson of mobilising her reserves of physical strength almost to a count-down of seconds. At Pasadena during a seminar which went on far too long she said to me under her breath, "Larry, I have about eleven minutes before I must simply lie down or collapse; let us wind this up. Don't worry, Rupert will be there to fix me up." And of course you were there. Meanwhile she had lectured and answered questions for nearly two hours, greeted students, performed several small acts of spontaneous kindness to timid pupils—in fact nobody could have noticed how ill she was, so splendid was her beauty and her bearing.

Her work is there now for us to read, in many languages, and her role in the modern world is a fruitful one. She taught that women must put a high price on themselves and demand the right to be free, but that in doing so they should not lose their femininity—for the whole civilised world of good values upon which our children will depend for their growth and mental well-being is precisely the work of the feminine element. And a world without real women in it to guide and nourish and inform its values will fall apart.

I am so happy to have lived in the same small moment of time with her; and I hardly dare to mourn her death—I seem to see that mischievous small smile with its sardonic edge, and hear that quiet laugh.

Larry

Letter from Rupert Pole to Lawrence Durrell:
Los Angeles, March 2, 1977

Dear Larry,

Please forgive this late reply but as you will see, I am drowned in work.

So good of you to take time to write such an eloquent eulogy. Unfortunately, it arrived on the 22nd (there was no mail on 20th—Sunday, or 21st—a holiday) too late to be read at the program. But perhaps this is better because International College would like to print it and send it out to people who send donations to the A.N. scholarship. I assume you will not object to this. Also I'm sure you won't mind if I edit slightly—just to delete your generous references to me. Some will undoubtedly find their way to New York and I don't think Hugo is ready for this yet. However, we have been corresponding and I'm sure Anaïs will be delighted if we can ultimately achieve an empathetic relationship.

The mood of the program was just right—a charming, low-key jazz combo [...] composed a piece for the occasion, *The Lady of the Houseboat.* You would have loved the soft, inventive piano and the Cuban drumming, and Balinese sounds of the bamboo windchimes would have delighted Anaïs (her name for the two of us was "Lord and Lady Windchime"). Christopher Isherwood was reticent and just right as moderator; Stephen Spender read three short, wonderful poems; Anaïs's students talked about Anaïs as a teacher; I broke the tension by getting people to laugh and showed slides (from the diaries) of A. 3 months to 20 and then zany slides from our travels. Henry couldn't make it (he had a bad fall recently) but I read two charming pages he wrote as a preface to a photobook titled "Anaïs Nin, Venus Anadyomene."[143] Program ended with the [Robert] Snyder film [*Anaïs Nin Observed*] which is like a visit with Anaïs at our home.

---

[143] On April 24, 1977, *The New York Times* described H.M.'s tribute as "a luminous, loving appraisal, and personal memoir, of Anaïs Nin as archetype of femininity and Feminism."

Working terribly hard—but of course it is the best thing [...] Anaïs has given me my life's work—and I am so grateful—I would be lost now if I tried to go back to teaching.[144]

A few joyous thoughts for you and Ghislaine. In 1966 Anaïs was in the hospital facing crucial surgery. The galleys of *Diary 1* were brought to her. She prayed that she might live long enough to know the reaction to the diary. [...] Anaïs was able to see the reaction to six volumes of diaries, to carry on a love affair with the world through the writing, lectures and correspondence and to fulfill her lifelong dream of being a roving reporter even though she finally had roots here in our beautiful house. "I have transportable roots," she once wrote! In her beloved Bali she wrote: "I made a wish: Let me think of death as a flight to another life, a joyous transformation, a release of our spirit so it might visit all other lives." Whenever we need her, her spirit will be with us.

Thank you both for the moving telegram and thank Ghislaine for her beautiful letter...

Love to you both,
Rupert

---

[144] A.N. had designated R.P. as her literary executor and Trustee of the Anaïs Nin Trust.

Appendix

1. Lawrence Durrell's seminar notes

From January to March 1974, Lawrence Durrell lectured at CalTech; Anaïs Nin joined him for his final talk, which was on D.H. Lawrence's *Sons and Lovers*. These are his notes from that evening:

Last Seminar

CALIFORNIA INSTITUTE OF TECHNOLOGY

PASADENA CALIFORNIA 91109   **16 March 1974**

DIVISION OF THE HUMANITIES
AND SOCIAL SCIENCES

WE HAVE A RIGHT TO TAKE A LOOK AT THE NOVEL IN TERMS OF BIOGRAPHY BECAUSE DL SUPPLIED THE DATA AND HIMSELF DID NOT SHRINK FROM THE MAIN THEME OF MOTHER FIXATION . BUT THEIR ARE NUMEROUS THUMB PRINTS ON THE TEXT . FIRST JESSIE CHAMBERS AS MIRIAM BASIS OF THE BATTLE HIS MOTHER WON . BUT FRIEDA WAS OF DIFFERENT STUFF . WEEKLY . MARRIED TWO CHILDREN WRENCH . BOTH WROTE BITS, BOTH GUIDED DHL IN THE LIGHT OF THEIR FEELINGS. THE THIRD WAS A COMPOSITE OF SEVERAL BUT SHE IS PRAISED FOR ALL THE QUALITIES WE HAVE LEARNED TO SEE IN FRIEDA WHO WAS ALREADY ON THE SCENE, KNEW ALL ABOUT MOTHER FIXATION AND TRANSFERENCE AND TRIED TO TEACH THE RECALCITRANT DHL A BIT WITHOUT RESULT IN MY VIEW.

```
MIRIAM    (Jessie Chambers)        FRIEDA WEEKLY
BAS BLEU                           living in sin
STICK                              two children
INTELLECTUAL                       sex knickers etc RAldington
SEX REFUSAL          CLARA         pyjamas  Compton Macenzie
                                     Frieda and Tropic .
```

BUT WE MUST NOT FORGET RICHARD GARNETT THE MENTOR WHO FINALLY PRUNED AN OVERLOADED TEXT WHICH STILL HASN'T BEEN PRINTED IN FULL. HE ALSO PERSUADED DHL TO DROP THE WELSH BAPTIST PREFACE.

POPULARISATION AND VULGARISATION OF PSYCHOANALYSIS IN PRESS HAS SPREAD A LOT OF MISINFORMATION : A COMPLEX IS NOT SOMETHING LIKE A NON FILTERABLE VIRUS. THE MAJORITY OF MOTHER FIXATION TYPES AND HELPED BY MUM TO SURMOUNT THE FIX AND MUM PUSHES THEM INTO THE MAIN STREAM OR THROWS THEM IN THE DEEP END WHEN THE CRITICAL MOMENT APPROACHES. MUM KNEW ALL ABOUT TRANSFERENCE LONG BEFORE FREUD. THE MOTHER'S WHO REALLY BEHAVE LIKE PRAYING MANTISES ARE THEMSELVES GRAVELY WOUNDED SOMEWHERE MOSTLY ALWAYS IN THE FAILURE OF THEIR MARRIAGE AND OFTEN SEXWISE.

```
FIRST DHL PORTRAIT OF THE FAMILY      FAMILY.        I4   I5
DHL DESCRIPTION OF THE BOOK           PAUL MOREL     I8   I9
   FRIEDA ON DHL                      FRIEDS
   MIRIAMS RIPOSTE..                  MIRIAM
```

Visit of Anais Nin to seminar.
   Introduce Anais   PREFACE
                      page 22.
                      complexes32
Paper Chase across literature of last 50 yrs
Trace the Zeitgeist spirit of the age -
Come to rest on 'SOnS and Lovers'.

2. Lawrence Durrell's preface to *Children of the Albatross*

Note: This is the final, edited version used in the 1959 Peter Owen edition.

It is good to be able to welcome Anaïs Nin's work to England at last, for she is a writer of real force who has established her own private kingdom in contemporary literature and who has remained too long in the wilderness. I have always thought of her as belonging to the great subjective-feminine tradition (Virginia Wololf, Djuna Barnes, Anna Kavan) which has tried to give us a poetic notation o the female artist's world. Though widely different in temperament and personality, the literary tradition these writers have established seems to me to be distinguished by one common factor: none wishes to transcribe reality in objective terms but to extract its essence—the shifting, sliding parcel of intuitions which each single second must present to the attention of a poet becoming aware of the true mainsprings of consciousness.

Anaïs Nin's highly distilled prose, which has the sort of rhythm and accent of poetry, does precisely this; her books are iridescent, held together by a finely-spun web of cross-references. Their preoccupation is with poetic truth and the human personality, not in terms of rigid objective valuations but in terms of symbol. Their subjectivity demands complete surrender in the reader, without which the spell will not have a chance to work. Gerard de Nerval's *Sylvie* demands as much, and rewards the reader in the same way.

The influence of circumstance and place cannot be discounted, and I think Anaïs Nin's native Spanishness of mind comes out in the highly charged impressionist palette with which she has chosen to work. American by nationality, Spanish by race, European by habit of mind and education—these are the ingredients which go to make up her style of mind, her inner attitudes.

But in the last analysis the work must speak for itself. Those who care for finely-wrought musical writing shot through with clear insights into the inner world of human beings will not be disappointed. She herself describes her work as "tapestry" and I think no more exact word will do.

INDEX

Index

Index

147

BIBLIOGRAPHY

Chamberlin, Brewster. *The Durrell Log: A Chronology of the Life and Times of Lawrence Durrell*. London: Colenso Books, 2019.

Durrell, Lawrence and Henry Miller. *The Durrell-Miller Letters, 1935-80*. New York: New Directions, 1988. (DML)

Nin, Anaïs. *The Diary of Anaïs Nin, Volume Two, 1934-1939*. New York: Harcourt Brace & World/The Swallow Press, 1967. (D2)

----. *The Diary of Anaïs Nin, Volume Three, 1939-1944*. New York: Harcourt Brace Jovanovich, 1969.

----. *The Diary of Anaïs Nin, Volume Six, 1955-1966*. New York: Harcourt Brace Jovanovich, 1976.

----. *The Diary of Anaïs Nin, Volume Seven, 1966-1974*. New York: Harcourt Brace Jovanovich, 1980.

----. *Nearer the Moon: The Previously Unpublished, Unexpurgated Diary, 1937-1939*. New York: Harcourt Brace & Company, 1996. (Moon)

Stuhlmann, Gunther (ed.). *ANAIS: An International Journal*, Volume 5. Los Angeles: The Anaïs Nin Foundation, 1987. (AIJ5)

ALSO AVAILABLE FROM SKY BLUE PRESS

Reunited: The Correspondence of Anaïs and Joaquín Nin 1933-1940 by Anaïs Nin and Joaquín Nin (print, ebook)

Auletris: Erotica by Anaïs Nin (print, ebook, audiobook)

Trapeze: The Unexpurgated Diary of Anaïs Nin, 1947-1955 by Anaïs Nin (print, ebook)

Mirages: The Unexpurgated Diary of Anaïs Nin, 1939-1947 by Anaïs Nin (print, ebook)

The Portable Anaïs Nin by Anaïs Nin, ed. Benjamin Franklin V (print, ebook)

D.H. Lawrence: An Unprofessional Study by Anaïs Nin (ebook)

House of Incest by Anaïs Nin (ebook)

The Winter of Artifice: 1939 Paris Edition by Anaïs Nin (print, ebook)

Under a Glass Bell by Anaïs Nin (ebook)

Stella by Anaïs Nin (ebook)

Ladders to Fire by Anaïs Nin (ebook)

Children of the Albatross by Anaïs Nin (ebook)

The Four-Chambered Heart by Anaïs Nin (ebook)

A Spy in the House of Love by Anaïs Nin (ebook)

Seduction of the Minotaur by Anaïs Nin (ebook)

Cities of the Interior by Anaïs Nin (ebook)

Collages by Anaïs Nin (ebook)

The Novel of the Future by Anaïs Nin (ebook)

Anaïs Nin: The Last Days, a Memoir by Barbara Kraft (ebook)

Anaïs Nin's Lost World: Paris in Words and Pictures 1924-1939 by Britt Arenander (print, ebook)

Anaïs Nin Character Dictionary and Index to Diary Excerpts by Benjamin Franklin V (print, ebook)

A Café in Space: The Anaïs Nin Literary Journal, Vol. 1 by Anaïs Nin, Janet Fitch, Lynette Felber... (print, ebook)

A Café in Space: The Anaïs Nin Literary Journal, Vol. 2 by Anaïs Nin, Benjamin Franklin V, Masako Meio... (print, ebook)

A Café in Space: The Anaïs Nin Literary Journal, Vol. 3 by Anaïs Nin, Gunther Stuhlmann, Richard Pine, James Clawson... (print, ebook)

A Café in Space: The Anaïs Nin Literary Journal, Vol. 4 by Anaïs Nin, Alan Swallow, John Ferrone, Yuko Yaguchi... (print, ebook)

A Café in Space: The Anaïs Nin Literary Journal, Vol. 5 by Anaïs Nin, Duane Schneider, Sarah Burghauser... (print, ebook)

A Café in Space: The Anaïs Nin Literary Journal, Vol. 6 by Anaïs Nin, Joaquín Nin y Castellanos, Tristine Rainer, Christie Logan... (print, ebook)

A Café in Space: The Anaïs Nin Literary Journal, Vol. 7 by Anaïs Nin, John Ferrone, Kim Krizan, Tristine Rainer...

A Café in Space: The Anaïs Nin Literary Journal, Vol. 8 by Anaïs Nin, Benjamin Franklin V, Anita Jarczok, Kim Krizan... (print, ebook)

A Café in Space: The Anaïs Nin Literary Journal, Vol. 9 by Anaïs Nin, Anita Jarczok, Joel Enos... (print, ebook)

A Café in Space: The Anaïs Nin Literary Journal, Vol. 10 by Anaïs Nin, Benjamin Franklin V, Kim Krizan, William Claire, Erin Dunbar... (print, ebook)

A Café in Space: The Anaïs Nin Literary Journal, Vol. 11 by Anaïs Nin, Henry Miller, Alfred Perlès, John Tytell... (print, ebook)

A Café in Space: The Anaïs Nin Literary Journal, Vol. 12 by Anaïs Nin, Kim Krizan, Benjamin Franklin V... (print, ebook)

A Café in Space: The Anaïs Nin Literary Journal, Vol. 13 by Anaïs Nin, Barbara Kraft, Danica Davidson... (print, ebook)

A Café in Space: The Anaïs Nin Literary Journal, Vol. 14 by Anaïs Nin, Jessica Gilbey, Joaquín Nin-Culmell... (print, ebook)

A Café in Space: The Anaïs Nin Literary Journal, Vol. 15 by Anaïs Nin, Rupert Pole, Steven Reigns... (print, ebook)

A Café in Space: The Anaïs Nin Literary Journal, Anthology 2003-2018 (print, ebook)

Forthcoming:

The Diary of Others: The Unexpurgated Diary of Anaïs Nin, 1955-1966

A Joyous Transformation: The Unexpurgated Diary of Anaïs Nin, 1966-1977